MW00466938

RESTORING
THE
AMERICAN DREAM

RESTORING
THE
AMERICAN DREAM

★ ★ ★

by

Michel J. Faulkner

Unless otherwise identified, all Scripture quotations in this publication are taken from the New American Standard Bible® (NASB), Copyright © 1960, 1962, 1963, 1968, 1971, 1972, 1973, 1975, 1977, 1995 by The Lockman Foundation. Used by permission.

Scripture quotations marked (NIV) are taken from the *Holy Bible, New International Version*®. NIV®. Copyright © 1973, 1978, 1984 by International Bible Society. Used by permission of Zondervan Publishing House. All rights reserved.

Restoring the American Dream
ISBN 978-1-936314-30-0
Copyright © 2010 by Michel J. Faulkner

Published and distributed by: Camden House Books
P.O. Box 701403
Tulsa, Oklahoma 74170

Printed in the United States of America. All rights reserved under International Copyright Law. Contents and/or cover may not be reproduced in whole or in part in any form without the express written consent of the Publisher, except for brief quotations in critical reviews or articles.

DEDICATION

I dedicate this book to my wife, Virginia, who is my soul mate and best friend. After more than 27 years of marriage, her love and support, as well as her personal experiences in coming to America, continue to be God's gifts to me.

And to my mother, Queenita Gaskins, whose strength and commitment to the American Dream shaped and molded me when it mattered most. You are the most wonderful example of God's grace.

CONTENTS

FOREWORD

It's funny how things happen. I grew up in a working-class, Bronx, New York, family as a die-hard New York Jets fan. Even though the Giants played nearby at Yankee Stadium, we relished watching the scrappy, blue collar Jets beat up on their opponents (and many times taking a beating themselves).

Years later, after I became a financial media regular for a number of uncannily accurate (and highly unpopular) stock market predictions, I met the man who would change my mind and have me root for the Giants, too. That man was former running back and two–time Super Bowl Champion New York Giant Lee Rouson. Lee and I co-founded Trinity Financial Sports & Entertainment Management Co., LLC, and through that company I met many other athletes, sports legends, and celebrities.

It was Lee who introduced me to Reverend Michel Faulkner, a man I have come to respect very much. Faulkner was a college standout at Virginia Tech who played for the Jets until he was sidelined by injury. Lee and Michel didn't care what color jersey the other was wearing when they teamed up for the non-profit organization "IFL—Institute for Leadership," whose mission was to develop leadership skills in youth. And I was pleased to help them.

I got to know Michel better through his different ministries, and I have come to truly admire his integrity, vision, and sincere desire to serve people. This is a man who is an overcomer. He rose above the obstacles of growing up as the child of a single working mom to attend a top-rated university; he triumphed by playing in the NFL against all odds, despite an injury and his small stature; he prevailed by returning to college and earning his master's degree after his NFL career was over; and he has made a difference on the streets of New York through a number of very successful ministries that have changed countless lives.

Now Michel Faulkner is up against another obstacle—taking on career-politician Charles Rangel for the opportunity to serve his Harlem neighbors in the United States Congress. Though each of us likely has a different vision of the American Dream, Michel Faulkner's *Restoring the American Dream* is universal to all of us. It's about hope and courage; family and country; commitment and service. He explores the origins of the Dream and what it means to so many different Americans, and he reveals how the creation of jobs and not compromising on our ideals will allow all of us to overcome.

Faulkner states quite clearly the root of the problem: ". . . The present climate of greed and corruption amongst our business and political leaders (now more quickly and thoroughly exposed through instant reporting) as well as a fundamental shift in ideology away from individual freedoms, is undermining the structural fabric essential for the survival of the American Dream—for this generation and perhaps also for all future generations."

That's a powerful statement, and frankly, why I became involved in this project. Faulkner explains how it is up to each of us—black, white, Latino, Asian and everything in between—to fight for the American Dream that our grandfathers and great-grandfathers fought for; to make our country better for the next generation by ensuring that the morals and foundation upon which this great nation was founded are left intact for our children and their children; to hold these truths and others to be self-evident: that all men and women are created equal.

The readers of my Grandich.com blog know that I don't pull punches. I speak my mind whether it's politically correct to do so or not. If I disagree with you, I'll say it. And when I find someone who is the "real deal"—a true American hero fighting for the rights of others—I will say that, too. That's Michel Faulkner—a bona fide, honest, caring, and loyal American who wants nothing but to serve the great people of New York. I am thrilled to have been a part of this project because I believe it will help not just his fellow New Yorkers understand where our nation is headed and get back on track, but it will aid all peace-loving people to get a closer look at the ideals upon which America was founded . . . and where we are going astray.

Michel sums up why he wrote the book, why I am recommending it, and why every American should read it: *"I have always believed that my highest calling in life is to serve the powerless and to speak for the voiceless."* That's the kind of guy who would pen a book teaching us all how to regain our dream and recast the American spirit. I am so pleased to be associated with this project.

PETER GRANDICH

Founder, Grandich Publications and Editor of The Grandich Letter *at www.Grandich.com*

Founder, Trinity Financial Sports & Entertainment Management Co.

EDITOR'S NOTE

By Long time Michel Faulkner friend Richard Groberg, who assisted Michel is writing and editing this book.

When, according to Michel: *"I came to New York to try out for the Jets as a defensive lineman...I was considered the '2-2 player'. I was too short and too slow. In spite of all of those obstacles, at the end of the training camp I was still there. I was able to overcome great odds to be a part of the Jets. I have always overcome the odds to achieve the impossible"*.

That's what some are saying about Michel's current attempt to win the 15th Congressional Seat, held for the last 40 years by Democrat Charles Rangel. *"Rangel can't be beat and this district is 80% democratic"*, some say. Michel believes in the American Dream and that, because of that, in this country anything is possible. *"I have always believed that my highest calling is to serve the powerless and to speak for the voiceless. I will bring that same energy and drive as your representative in Washington, D.C."*

His goals with regard to this book and his candidacy are to wake us up to the daily dismantling of the American Dream and the risk it poses for this and future generations. Michel's message is important for all to hear.

ACKNOWLEDGEMENTS

From start to finish, *Restoring the American Dream* has been an amazing project. I would like to begin by thanking God, who has given me the strength and stamina to complete this leg of my journey. His guidance, comfort, and daily miracles have continued to be the most amazing experiences of my life.

I would like to thank Peter Grandich for your faith in God and love for our nation. I wish there were more people like you who were willing to put their money where their mouth is. You are the best.

Next, I would like to thank Jo Schloeder, whose friendship and artistry serve as a wonderful reminder of God's creativity.

Thank you Howard Ryan for believing in me and this book when very few did. I will ever be in your debt.

To my son, Michel, my prayer is that we would have many other opportunities for collaboration. Your skills and expertise continued to amaze me.

Thanks to Richard Groberg, whose friendship over the past 20 years and collaboration on this book are true gifts from God. It goes without saying that none of this would have happened without you.

CHAPTER 1

THE BIRTH OF
THE DREAM

*"We hold these truths to be self-evident, that all men are
created equal, that they are endowed by their Creator
with certain unalienable rights, that among these are life,
liberty and the pursuit of happiness."*

—THE DECLARATION OF INDEPENDENCE, 1776

The United States has been built and sustained largely by
the pursuit of what we commonly call the "American Dream":
life, liberty, and the pursuit of happiness. The very founding
of the United States was initiated by the early Americans'

rebellion against oppression and the suppression of individual rights by the British government. In fact, the two most important governing documents of our country, the Declaration of Independence and the Constitution, were crafted to ensure and protect those very rights.

Unfortunately, the present climate of greed and corruption amongst our business and political leaders (now more quickly and thoroughly exposed through instant reporting) as well as a fundamental shift in ideology away from individual freedoms, is undermining the structural fabric essential for the survival of the American Dream—for this generation and perhaps also for all future generations.

EVERY GENERATION OF AMERICANS MUST FIGHT FOR DEMOCRACY TO SECURE THE FUTURES OF THEIR CHILDREN.

My perspective is that of an American citizen and not that of a professional politician or commentator. But it is my hope to appeal to all who love America and believe that the American Dream can still become a reality, to step up and rally against this frightening prospect. John Adams, second President of the United States, once said, "I must study politics and war, that my sons have liberty to study mathematics and philosophy." What I believe he meant was that every generation of Americans must fight for democracy to secure the futures of their children.

THE BIRTH OF THE DREAM
★ ★ ★

In Search of Life, Liberty, and Happiness

Democracy is not easy and it is not free. It requires work. Because our government was established with a balance of power between its three branches, and because it is a government "of the people, by the people, and for the people," it requires continued refinement and effort to maintain and grow it in adherence to the principles it was founded on. It requires that each generation do its part. And while every generation has its own struggles, it seems that currently, while we all see the unraveling of the fabric of our society and the pervasive corruption that is choking our nation, this current generation seems less inclined than prior ones to step forward and attempt to do something about it.

The *"American Dream,"* a well-known term to citizens and non-citizens alike, was first coined in 1931 by J.T. Adams (1878-1949), U.S. writer and historian, in *Epic of America:* "[The American Dream is] that dream of a land in which life should be better and richer and fuller for everyone, with opportunity for each according to ability or achievement. It is a difficult dream for the European upper classes to interpret adequately, and too many of us ourselves have grown weary and mistrustful of it. It is not a dream of motor cars and high wages merely, but a dream of social order in which each man and each woman shall be able to attain to the fullest stature of which they are innately capable, and be recognized by others for what they are, regardless of the fortuitous circumstances of birth or position."[1]

This idea has exhibited itself throughout our history. From the beginning, people have come to the United States looking for a better life, liberty, and the freedom to pursue individual happiness. America provides ". . . to every man, regardless of his birth, his shining, golden opportunity . . . the right to live, to work, to be himself, and to become whatever thing his manhood and his vision can combine to make him," (Thomas Wolfe).

In pursuit of these inalienable rights, homesteaders left the big cities of the east to find happiness and their piece of land in the unknown wilderness of the west. After the Civil War, freed slaves sought to make their own way and build a better, brighter future. Veterans of World War II sought to settle down and have a home, a car, and a family. The suffragette of the early 1900s sought equal rights for women. Martin Luther King Jr. and Malcolm X sought equality for blacks. And since the birth of our great country, hopeful immigrants from every nation have come to the United States in search of these same inalienable rights—applying their skills to make a better life.

The liberties that we enjoy and pursue as Americans can only be protected as we mutually respect the rule of law. There are many interpretations of the rule of law, but one definition is that there is a "higher law"—a code of ethics and behavior that is supported and enforced by each citizen. The rule of law protects us from anarchy by providing the means to address grievances without violence.

Unfortunately, our form of democracy, as embodied in the ideal that we can exist as a sovereign and independent nation of hard-working, peace-loving people, becomes insupportable if Americans don't believe in it anymore. As Americans, we expect our business leaders to be aggressive and our politicians to be passionate. We don't expect or demand moral perfection from either. However, when we see such widespread greed and corruption go unchecked, it undermines the very fabric of our nation. It undermines our confidence and faith in the dream that is bred in the hearts of Americans. When we become apathetic about democracy, democracy will not work—in the United States or abroad.

The Corruption of Democracy

We are not the first generation to struggle with the preservation of the American Dream. Since our nation's inception, our leaders have been torn by the inevitable conflict between the fruits of power and conscience. The most prevalent of these conflicts related to the practice of slavery. Until

★ SINCE OUR NATION'S INCEPTION, OUR LEADERS HAVE BEEN TORN BY THE INEVITABLE CONFLICT BETWEEN THE FRUITS OF POWER AND CONSCIENCE.

the Civil War, our nation and its leaders struggled with the implications of years of compromise. Leaders often found themselves trying to reconcile themselves to policies with respect to slavery that were contrary to the American Dream.

For many, there was an economic benefit to slavery. However, even before the Civil War, prominent leaders struggled with the fact that they could not act as moral beacons with slavery "skeletons" in their respective closets. They constantly wrestled with questions such as, "Does the end justify the means?" and "Are all men truly created equal?" Even two of our most well known forefathers, Thomas Jefferson and George Washington, wrestled with the slavery question.

Greed and corruption aren't new inventions either. From biblical times through the modern era, recorded history has story after story of leaders consumed and often toppled because of their greed and corruption. We have struggled with these vices in the United States since its inception; however, many believe that rarely before have they been so widespread, so accepted and deeply entrenched in the culture of our nation—especially in our elected lawmakers. There are so many examples, not just amongst political leaders, but also business leaders and clergy, that we could devote an entire book just to summarizing and analyzing them.

However, even though it seems as though "everyone is doing it," that cannot justify this behavior. Nor does it mean that we should accept such conduct in our leaders. President John Adams once said, "Because power corrupts, society's demands for moral authority and character increase as the importance of the position increases."

I am not suggesting that today's leaders are worse than those of the past, or that the problem is more pervasive. What is apparent is that our common adherence to the rule of law seems to be diminishing. In this age of instant information, more people hear bad news and reports of corruption, often seemingly in "real time." The next result is that the age of instant information has led to an era of complacency. The assumption and acceptance of greed, misplaced or not, is creating a growing disconnect between Americans and the foundational moral presuppositions that have been and will continue to be essential for our democracy to function.

Without the general belief that the laws and principles of the United States provide *all* United States citizens the opportunity to get ahead by working hard, America cannot function as intended. When the American people do not act with conviction to defend a system that attempts to protect the rights of citizens from arbitrary and abusive use of government power, our Constitution is in very real jeopardy.

> "BECAUSE POWER CORRUPTS, SOCIETY'S DEMANDS FOR MORAL AUTHORITY AND CHARACTER INCREASE AS THE IMPORTANCE OF THE POSITION INCREASES."
> —JOHN ADAMS

Taking A Stand

Some Americans are resigned to the belief that all leaders are in the political arena only for personal gain, and therefore getting involved is a lost cause. Others, however, are stepping up, just as the American colonists did in the mid-1700s against British tyranny.

> WE NEED A REVOLUTION . . . NOT ONLY OF CHANGE, BUT OF HONESTY; A REVOLUTION OF INTEGRITY IN WHICH WE HOLD EVERY AMERICAN ACCOUNTABLE FOR THEIR ACTIONS.

A prominent example of those taking a stand is the Tea Party Movement, which began organizing a series of nationally coordinated protests throughout the United States in 2009. The Tea Party's website defines their cause as, "A community committed to standing together, shoulder to shoulder, to protect our country and the Constitution upon which we were founded!" Their self-professed mission is ". . . to attract, educate, organize, and mobilize our fellow citizens to secure public policy consistent with our three core values of Fiscal Responsibility, Constitutionally Limited Government, and Free Markets."[2]

American democracy will work if there is a sincere, well-placed confidence in the honesty and integrity of our leaders and in the fairness and equity of those who govern our nation. To combat the downward spiral, we need a revolution—a revolution not only of change, but of honesty; a revolution of integrity in which we hold every American accountable for their actions—from the highest levels of government to the everyday lives of private citizens. We cannot survive as a nation of thieves.

One of the more painful realities of our current political climate is the fact that among young Americans, faith in the American Dream is hard to come by. The trust and idealism of the generation who must carry the dream forward has been betrayed by the obvious greed and corruption that pervades our society. People who don't believe in the American Dream don't trust democracy. People who don't trust democracy don't vote—or they vote for candidates and ideals against democracy.

It is time for a wake up call! Our generation must understand that the American Dream is in danger of being lost—perhaps forever. We have to restore faith in the basic American ideals of justice, honesty, civility, and integrity. We have to restore faith in the American Dream. We must do it for ourselves and for our children and for our children's children.

This is what has motivated me for more than twenty years to take a stand and serve others as a minister and community leader in Harlem, and hopefully, going forward as Upper Manhattan's voice in the House of Representatives.

CHAPTER 2

ONE MAN'S DREAM

"The poorest man is not the one without a cent,
but the one without a dream."

—AUTHOR UNKNOWN

I have always believed that my highest calling in life is to serve the powerless and to speak for the voiceless. Not because I have all the answers, but because I have walked in their shoes.

I was born on May 21, 1957, in Baltimore, Maryland, to Queenita Hairston, a 21-year-old single working mother. I grew up barely knowing my biological father, and although my mother later married and my stepfather adopted me, their marriage ended in divorce when I was eleven years old. As a result, I grew up without any consistent interaction with a trusted father figure.

But like so many other young boys in similar circumstances, I channeled my energy into competitive athletics. The same year my parents divorced, I began playing football for the local police boys' club. Then, during my sophomore year in high school, I became a regular starter on the varsity football team. I eventually went on to become a freshman All-American defensive lineman at Virginia Tech while I was working toward my B.A. in communications and sociology. Balancing a grueling practice schedule and academics, my college years were a valuable lesson in the importance of working hard to achieve my goals.

Tests and Trials

During my junior year at Virginia Tech, I suffered a major knee injury and was red-shirted in 1977. But I was determined to play football again, and after making a full recovery, I returned to finish my eligibility in 1979. Then came the greatest challenge of my athletic career: I traveled to New York to try out for the New York Jets as a defensive lineman. At that time, the Jets already had four all-pro defensive linemen. Also, they had drafted three defensive lineman that year, and, as if that wasn't enough, they had also signed two other free agents—both of whom had prior NFL training camp experience.

Of all those linemen, I was considered the "2-2 player." I was too short and too slow. But in spite of all obstacles, at the end of training camp I was still there. I played one season in the NFL. And while my pro football career only lasted one year, I was able to overcome great odds to be a part of the Jets.

> ★ I WAS THE
> ★ "2-2 PLAYER."
> I WAS TOO
> ★ SHORT AND TOO
> ★ SLOW. BUT IN
> SPITE OF ALL
> ★ OBSTACLES, AT
> ★ THE END OF
> TRAINING CAMP
> ★ I WAS STILL
> ★ THERE.

Achieving the seemingly impossible by playing professional football was a valuable lesson that I quickly had to draw strength from. In early 1982, I returned home and began looking for employment. Like so many Americans today, at that time I was unemployed and facing a rough economy and bleak job prospects. In order to help my mother, who was struggling to pay her mortgage and other bills, I worked multiple menial jobs.

Answering the Call

Led in part by the encouragement and guidance of a trusted pastor, in 1983 I returned to Virginia Tech to earn a master's degree in education and career counseling. Upon completion of my degree in 1985, I met the Reverend Jerry Falwell and soon after became the Assistant Dean of

Students at Liberty University. It wasn't long before I was promoted to the role of Vice President for Urban Ministry in 1987.

I traveled the nation meeting many prominent black pastors such as Dr. Tony Evans, Dr. John Perkins, and Tom Skinner. Among them was the late E.V. Hill, famed civil rights leader and pastor to Hollywood stars in the 70s and 80s. I was fortunate to meet many of the great Christian leaders of that era and they all mentored me in one way or another. During my time at Liberty, I trained, equipped, and sent out more than 100 urban missionaries who worked to feed the poor and provide for their basic needs—changing the lives of countless people in cities all across America.

I BEGAN TO FEEL A BURNING DESIRE TO WORK IN A MORE HANDS-ON WAY WITH THE INNER-CITY POOR AND DISADVANTAGED —SPECIFICALLY IN NEW YORK.

Because of my experiences at Liberty, working with inner-city ministries around the country, I began to feel a burning desire to work in a more hands-on way with the inner-city poor and disadvantaged—specifically in New York. So, in 1988, I returned to New York City to accept the role of Assistant Pastor and Director of The Lamb's Church in Times Square.

The Lamb's Church was different than any of the other churches I'd been involved with before. I had the privilege of serving the poor at welfare hotels and soup kitchens. But just three months after I had joined the staff, a social worker and director of The Lamb Center resigned. The pastor approached me and asked me if I wouldn't mind helping out until they could find a replacement. I loved the challenge—it was exactly what I needed to balance my "Ivory Tower" experience at Liberty University.

One year later, I joined Calvary Baptist Church in midtown Manhattan as Pastor for Youth and Community Outreach. My focus was on training and developing youth leaders and I also created and managed the church's programs serving the homeless, the prison ministry, and an HIV/AIDS program. A couple of years later, in December, 1991, I was ordained.

Then in 1993, I became the Senior Pastor of Central Baptist Church—located on the upper West Side of Manhattan, just south of Harlem. During my nearly 14-year tenure at Central Baptist Church, I played a leadership role in the creation of numerous city and leadership development programs. It was also during this time that I began to take a serious interest in New York City politics.

A New Direction

One day, at a focus group meeting, I met Rudolph Giuliani and we stayed in touch. When Giuliani subsequently began his mayoral campaign, one of Rudy's top advisers contacted me and asked me to take a significant role in the campaign. While I declined to take a visible role, I remained a trusted volunteer and supporter. Then, when Giuliani won that election, he offered me a position within his administration as Director of the Mayor's Office of Education.

THE MONEY DIDN'T MATTER. IT REALLY WAS ABOUT THE CALLING.

I was very flattered by the offer and actually accepted the job; but then during the vetting process I discovered that I could not maintain my status as Senior Pastor at Central Baptist, so I had to decline. I knew God had not called me to resign as Pastor of Central Baptist Church. The money didn't matter. It really was about the calling. Nevertheless, I continued to help the Giuliani administration as a volunteer and unofficial advisor.

It has been my honor to serve the people of New York City in numerous initiatives, including Mayor Giuliani's Task Force on Police Community Relations; as Commissioner of the City Charter Review initiative; as Co-Chairman for the New York City Board of Education's HIV/AIDS Task Force; and as Vice President for Community Government Relations at King's College from 1988 to 1992. I also served as Regional Chaplain for New York State Office of Family and Children Services.

Additionally, from June 2002 to February 2004, I served as World Vision's Director of U.S. Programs. World Vision is an international partnership of Christians whose mission work is focused on serving the poor and oppressed. I came on board just after 9/11, and World Vision had just finished a multi-million dollar recovery effort in New York City. They asked me to help build sustainable programs through the churches in New York City. One great program that we were able to implement was a youth initiative. We actually gave funding to eight local churches in New York City to assist them in providing a full-time youth worker. The various grants allowed us to distribute more than $1 million over a three year period of time.

In 2005, along with my wife, Virginia, and my friend, Franco Olmeda, I started the Institute for Leadership—a Harlem-based, non-profit organization focused on the development of leaders and leadership programs. This Institute endeavors to bring transformational leadership principles to all areas and marketplaces for teachers, business leaders, government officials, other public servants, sports coaches, and ministers. Our vision at the IFL is to make a better tomorrow by making better leaders today. We began working with leaders, mostly in the sports arena, to try to develop teams of supporters for various youth-oriented athletic endeavors. This proved to be more difficult than we anticipated, but we were asked to begin a project with a health foundation to create a statewide faith-based diabetes reduction program.

The program we created works in three phases—first by helping faith communities know how many of their members have diabetes and what the causes are. Then we help them manage their numbers through exercise, diet, and proper medical treatment. And finally, we help them reduce their numbers by healthier lifestyle choices and spreading the good news. While this program is still being developed, the early prospects are extremely promising. Presently, we have already worked with more than 40 congregations throughout New York State creating this pilot initiative.

In June 2006, I embarked on a new journey related to my continued passion toward the city, founding the New Horizon Church of New York in Harlem. New Horizon Church is a Christ-centered community that is empowering a new generation of leaders to worship God in Spirit and in Truth. We are fellowshipping with each other with *agape* love, and we are inspiring others to transform the marketplace through excellence in ministry. While staying true to the Scriptures as it relates to doctrine, we want to be truly relevant and viable to meet the growing needs of our culture and society. I believe that the Gospel has to transcend culture in order to transform lives, and New Horizon Church is based on that model.

CHAPTER 3

FOR EVERY GENERATION

"Democracy is based upon the conviction that there are extraordinary possibilities in ordinary people."

—HARRY EMERSON FOSDICK

Every generation of immigrants has come to the United States with a common bond—the belief that they can have their own share of the American Dream. That they can get a good job, practice the religion of their choice, obtain a good education for their children, maybe even own a business and, over time, improve their lot in life.

The American Dream has not only shaped the growth and development of America but other nations, governments, and cultures as well. The upward mobility of society, the ready accessibility of technology, and relatively inexpensive modes of transportation continue to expand our borders. America is not perfect, but the role that it plays in the lives of those who desire to be here continues to be perfected. For them, the American Dream is the goal . . . an ideal . . . a quest. At its best, the quest is a great venture into an uncertain future, yet the destination is a commonly held vision of all who dream of America—for a richer, fuller life built upon the content of one's character. We remain the only nation that has set this unique vision for all of its citizens and ahead of all other national aspirations.

THE AMERICAN DREAM IS THE GOAL . . . AN IDEAL . . . A QUEST.

Ideally, the roadmap to achieving the American Dream should be passed down from generation to generation. Each generation must do its part to advance the dream by tearing down obstacles for others and upholding the values and moral imperative before all other national considerations. This has been most difficult to maintain, especially during times of great national prosperity—of which we have had many, thanks to our country's free market system and the entrepreneurial zeal of Americans pursuing life, liberty, and happiness. We have forgotten that while the dream lies before us, it requires work and effort in order for the dream to be realized in our generation. One of the great disappointments of this generation has been that we have expected America to be America and have not been trained, equipped, or prepared to *work* for America to be America.

There is nothing "natural" about the American Dream. Mankind's natural inclination toward selfishness and callousness toward the needs of others—as well as our competitive nature—drives us to isolation, greed, and other practices aimed at getting ahead at the expense of others. That is the natural heart of man; all governments and societies established prior to the founding of America were built on some derivative of these principles.

But America's moral scope has been divinely inspired. As the Declaration of Independence reminds us, our founding fathers believed that our liberties were given to us by God and not by government. America was built by the people—working-class, merchant, slave, and gentry—all working together to achieve one dream. Faith in the American Dream means that, when laying down at the end of our days, we will be able to pass on to our children and our children's children these noble goals, ideals, and values.

> OUR LIBERTIES WERE GIVEN TO US BY GOD AND NOT BY GOVERNMENT.

Passing It On

Following the Great Depression and World War II, America's primary preoccupation was no longer the fight for freedom, but the security and prosperity of its citizens. This fostered in an age of unparalleled prosperity, as well as a failure on the part of the Baby Boomer generation to identify with some of the intrinsic principles of the American Dream. For many, the agreement and understanding that we must pass these principles on to our children was lost. There was also a failure to pass on the values of what it truly means to be an American.

An example of how values must be passed on to each generation can be found in the Bible. As Israel was preparing to go into the Promised Land, God commanded them not only to maintain the godly practice of ethics, but to pass them on to their children in perpetuity:

"Hear, O Israel! The LORD is our God, the LORD is one! You shall love the LORD your God with all your heart and with all your soul and with all your might. These words, which I am commanding you today, shall be on your heart. You shall teach them diligently to your sons and shall talk of them when you sit in your house and when you walk by the way and when you lie down and when you rise up. You shall bind them as a sign on your hand and they shall be as frontals on your forehead. You shall write them on the doorposts of your house and on your gates."

—Deuteronomy 6:4-9

It was God's purpose to establish an ongoing generational prosperity for Israel by having them always remember who they were and how they came into being. Their identity was about much more than being Jewish. Their identity came from being faithful subjects of the God of Israel. Their relationship to the God of Israel was not just an occurrence for a single generation—it would mark them as a unique and distinctive people for all generations. This was due in no small part to all that God had already done for them and still promised to do if they would worship him and pass on these traditions to their children and their children's children.

AMERICA'S CHILDREN HAVE GROWN UP WITH A SENSE OF ENTITLEMENT, WITHOUT BEING CHALLENGED TO TAKE ON THE WORK THAT IS NECESSARY TO ADVANCE AMERICA.

While America has been blessed by the Almighty God, we are not Israel. But we would do well to learn from the lessons God taught Israel during its national development. One of the most important lessons is to teach our children the values and moral suppositions that make America great. "Our Constitution was made only for a moral and religious people. It is wholly inadequate to the government of any other," (John Adams).

America's children have grown up with a sense of entitlement, without being challenged to take on the work that is necessary to advance America. We need to help our children understand that the ideal of the American Dream must be advanced by them. We need to teach our children that the rule of law and the legislative process continue to be inextricably bound to the prosperity of America. We must arm them with the ideas, understanding, and moral distinctives that have and will continue to make America the greatest nation on earth. Without passing on these ideas, based on the explicit direction given by those who have come before us, the ideal of the American Dream may die with this generation.

We will not all agree on the method or approach necessary to continue to grow, expand, and restore America. Be that as it may, we must determine to agree that the liberties you and I hold dear must be honored and protected by each generation.

Defending the Constitution

The Civil Rights era was a great movement in this country. Distinctly and uniquely American, it was a call for all people of our nation to live up to the ideals, goals, and values that make America great and that make the American Dream the envy of the world. The greatest leader of the Civil Rights Movement, Martin Luther King, Jr., is most known for his famous speech, aptly titled "I Have A Dream." King called upon the American people to stand up and defend the ideals and principles that our great country was founded upon: "I have a dream that one day this nation will rise up and live out the true meaning of its creed: 'We hold these truths to be self-evident: that all men are created equal.'"

I believe we have not given the children of this generation an understanding of the legislative process and about proper stewardship of the Constitution of the United States. If they do not have a working knowledge of the Constitution and an understanding of why it is critical to protect their personal freedoms, their children will know even less.

Remember, the ideals of America are not natural. The Declaration of Independence speaks of the inalienable rights of citizens endowed by the Creator. But if we have a generation that no longer understands what America is supposed to be about, nor believes that these rights are endowed by their Creator, they will no longer protect them and honor them as previous generations have.

This generation somehow thinks that the rights and privileges that we enjoy are given to us by the law or by the legislature or worse—by the legislators. None of these things are true. These liberties that we enjoy, that make up the American Dream, are endowed by our Creator and are given to us in a sacred trust—a covenant known as the Constitution and the Declaration of Independence.

CHAPTER 4

WHO STOLE THE DREAM?

"The American Dream does not happen by asking Americans to accept what's immoral and wrong in the name of tolerance."

—J.C. WATTS

The problem is that today, perhaps more than ever before in the United States, the average American feels powerless to impact and change the direction that our government is taking us. This separates Americans from democracy. And

THE AVERAGE AMERICAN FEELS POWERLESS TO IMPACT AND CHANGE THE DIRECTION THAT OUR GOVERNMENT IS TAKING US.

when Americans are separated from democracy, democracy does not work.

We have always had greed and corruption in the United States; such is the human condition. Unfortunately, too many of us believe that corruption has never been so widespread, so deeply entrenched in the culture of our nation, and therefore a "given" that we must accept—including from those we elect and appoint to govern and lead us.

Unfortunately, greed and corruption isn't a new characteristic among our leaders. In recent times we've witnessed the failings of Bill Clinton, John Edwards, Charles Sanford, John Ensign, Charles Rangel, and many others. But some of our most revered leaders, including some of our founding fathers, had their share of sexual and financial scandals. The personal lives of Thomas Jefferson, Aaron Burr, Ulysses S. Grant, Franklin Delano Roosevelt, John Kennedy and others were just as scandalous as those of our current generation of disgraced leaders.

Whether or not today's leaders are truly worse than those of the past, the age of instant information has led to the assumption by many that "every politician is corrupt." It seems that there is a new scandal breaking daily, often reported in real time.

Thomas Jefferson may have had torrid affairs while traveling in Europe, but such news could only find its way back to America via letter or word of mouth. Now, in this digital age, a mere text message can deliver news around the world instantaneously. Furthermore, digital cameras and cell phones transmit images and video instantly—often finding their way onto the internet and news forums just as quickly.

This assumption, misplaced or not, is creating a growing disconnect between Americans and the moral presuppositions that have been and will continue to be essential for our democracy to function. Without the general belief that the laws and principles of the United States provide anyone in the United States the opportunity to get ahead by working hard and that all are created equally, America cannot function as intended. Without a system that protects the rights of citizens from arbitrary and abusive use of government power, our very constitutional principles are in jeopardy.

Adhering to the belief or feeling that everyone in politics is greedy or corrupt, doesn't make it accurate. Nor does it mean that we should accept such behavior in our chosen leaders. Twentieth century business tycoon and part time politician Ross Perot once said, "If your wife can't trust you, how can your country?" Many have dismissed Perot's political aspirations, however, I believe he was right that our leaders must be held to a higher standard. How can we trust our leaders to protect the United States, to uphold the principals of the Declaration of Independence and the Constitution, and to protect our ability to achieve the American Dream if they are not men and women of integrity?

If a married president can be distracted from his political responsibilities in the White House to flirt with a teenage intern, what else was taking priority over his responsibilities to you and me? Aside from the moral implications, think about that same man making important political decisions minutes later. Think about what could have happened had that intern been used by nefarious parties to influence national policy. Some believe this actually happened during the Kennedy presidency. It just wasn't publicized as quickly and freely as today's transgressions.

A Lost Cause?

We are beginning to surrender to the erroneous belief that since our leaders are only in the political arena for personal gain, being involved is a lost cause. Voter turnout is down. Community activism is down. And other than the surge of volunteers during the Obama presidential campaign and the recent activity of the Tea Party movement, we don't see the same level of political activism as in past generations.

It is quite paradoxical that the largest segment of the U.S. population is the generation born between 1945 and 1958. This was the same generation that fueled the activist movements of the 1960s. Where are they now? Where are their children, now in their 30s and 40s? Why aren't they politically active? They did not learn that the price of liberty is high.

On the political landscape today, only the Tea Party seems to be rallying behind their message. Regardless of whether or not you agree with their beliefs, we all should applaud their efforts. They are actively involved in the political process. As a people and a nation, we cannot survive if we do not let our voices be heard.

WHERE ARE THEY NOW? WHERE ARE THEIR CHILDREN, NOW IN THEIR 30S AND 40S? WHY AREN'T THEY POLITICALLY ACTIVE?

★ ★ ★

CHAPTER 5

A NATION OF IMMIGRANTS

"Give me your tired, your poor,
Your huddled masses yearning to breathe free,
The wretched refuse of your teeming shore.
Send these, the homeless, tempest-tost to me,
I lift my lamp beside the golden door!"

—EMMA LAZARUS, FROM THE NEW COLOSSUS, 1883

The Statue of Liberty, and the above poem inscribed at its base, captures the philosophical paradigm of the American Dream: the United States has been built and sustained largely by immigrants and their pursuit of "life, liberty, and…happiness." The United States is a nation of immigrants and as such, immigrants have always been the lifeblood of our industrial and agricultural economy. Asian immigrants built our railroads, Irish and Italian immigrants built many buildings in the north, and slaves built most of our southern cities. But Lady Liberty's words also hearken back to the paradox of America's founding: it was fueled by rebellion against oppression and the suppression of individual rights by the British government.

The first two governing documents of our country, the Declaration of Independence and the Constitution, were crafted to guarantee and protect the rights of all who call this nation home. These documents also helped shape the role of our citizens and the continued improvement of our democracy. We must be a nation governed by rule of law. The first place where this is observed is in the immigration process. For this reason it is imperative that we secure our borders and our shores against those who come here illegally.

The sheer size and magnitude of our national government and social service delivery system demand that the influx of immigrants—though still the lifeblood of our nation—be controlled better than ever before. We cannot afford to provide for those who come to this country to take advantage rather than to contribute toward the common good. Otherwise, we impinge upon the room for the tired, the distressed, and the huddled masses who legitimately want to come to America to work hard, get ahead, and earn a piece of the American Dream for themselves and their children.

As I mentioned before, America is a nation of immigrants. Dr. Hasia Diner, professor of history at New York University in New York City, wrote, "Tens of millions of immigrants over four centuries have made the United States what it is today. They came to make new lives and livelihoods in the New World; their hard work benefited themselves and their new home country." America has more immigrants, both documented and undocumented, than any other nation in the world. And with each new wave of immigrants, the question of local or national acceptance has been tied to economics.

Because immigrants are often hard-pressed financially when first arriving in the United States, they historically have performed jobs other Americans wouldn't do, or accepted a significantly lower rate of pay than most Americans would demand. While this has angered the self-professed "real" Americans of each generation, the truth is that the nation was literally built by these immigrants who not only took those undesirable—yet integral—jobs, but willingly worked them for an hour longer and two dollars less.

Most of us have a story of a relative who came to the United States before us; or perhaps that of the circumstances of many African-Americans who moved from the rural South to the industrial North for better opportunities. They typically came with very little in the way of financial resources; worked hard; eventually sent word and money back to their relatives to join them; and over time, worked their way up from poverty, all the while becoming "an American." Every generation of immigrants has faced their own challenges and persecution; however, all were propelled by the belief in the sanctity of the American Dream.

AMERICA HAS MORE IMMIGRANTS, BOTH DOCUMENTED AND UNDOCUMENTED, THAN ANY OTHER NATION IN THE WORLD.

Each generation of immigrants sent in its "pioneers" to set the tempo and scout out the land. Then, when they were settled, they would send for their families, instilling in them a sense of purpose. These pioneers were the keepers of the American Dream because they gave those following after them an orientation speech about work and opportunity—and, more importantly, testified to what they already had achieved.

Lessons Learned

My wife came to this country from the Cape Verde Islands in 1966. Her grandfather, who had been a Merchant Marine, immigrated to the United States before World War II. When he and his wife first arrived, they immediately invested in property and started a business. This business would later become the beachhead and the foundational platform for the remainder of the family to immigrate.

My wife often tells the story of how she did not want to come to this country. As a young 11-year-old girl, this new place represented more work and less play. In addition, both of her parents immediately took jobs, which meant that she had to assume the role of caretaker for her younger siblings. But she quickly learned from the example of her parents and grandparents that hard work would reap a reward.

> ★
> ★
> ★
> ★
> ★
> WITH EACH JOB I WAS TOLD, "WORK HARD AND YOU WILL ADVANCE."

Certainly my wife's parents had to prepare their children for this new life and what was expected of them. I suspect that they gave a motivational "pep talk" as to why everyone had to shoulder these new responsibilities. And I imagine that this orientation speech was very similar to the one my mother gave me when it was time for me to get my first job outside my home. I was twelve years old and I began working after school and on the weekends for my mother—cleaning her beauty shop. By the time I was fourteen, I was helping with my grandmother's catering enterprise in Baltimore. At fifteen, I started helping my uncle the brick mason. With each job I was told, "work hard and you will advance."

My mother would often reinforce this message by giving me the "you can be anything you want to be" speech. A bit clichéd maybe, but nonetheless this valuable lesson and her example of hard work prepared me to go out into the world and pursue my dreams. My mother would tell me that, because I was black, I would have to learn to work twice as hard as the next guy if I wanted to get ahead.

It is very interesting to me today, when I reflect back on that time in my life, that my mother was never bitter about our blackness. Instead she radiated a quiet dignity and sense of pride—that she also tried to instill in me—in the fact that everything we had achieved was accomplished going uphill. She would tell me that, if I was willing to work twice as hard, eventually I would get ahead even if others wanted to hold me back.

I was told explicitly not to wait on anyone to give me an opportunity, but "to step up and speak up and make my own way." She also made it clear to me that, if I did these things, I would be able to get ahead because we lived in America and eventually laws would support our rise to freedom and the fulfillment of our own American Dream.

I am sure these themes were the same basic talking points of encouraging pep talks given by countless families—the working class Dutch, followed by the Jewish people, the Chinese, the Irish, the freed slaves, and the post-Vietnam war immigrants who came here from various parts of Southeast Asia. As a result, each generation of working-class

Americans entered the marketplace armed with a dream—the American Dream.

The immigrant, the poor, and the working class dared to believe that if they were able to work hard, they could get ahead—because they were in America. Some will say that this faith was based on the free market that needed and rewarded hard-working people. But I believe that it was more than that. I believe that it was confidence in the American Dream. They believed that one day they could own houses and property and businesses. Not a single one of them thought about being taken care of by the government or a government-run program.

The Role of Government

There is an important distinction between the working class and the ruling class in America. The working class does not own anything except their labor or skills as tradesmen. The ruling class would use the working class to further their own cause. With each wave of immigration, there were those of the ruling class who would take advantage of the dreams of the working class. Not everyone—but many.

WHENEVER THE VALUES AND WORTH OF THE WORKING CLASS ARE DEVALUED BY THE PREDATORY ACTIONS OF OTHERS, A PIECE OF THE AMERICAN DREAM IS STOLEN.

RESTORING THE AMERICAN DREAM
★ ★ ★

Whenever the values and worth of the working class are devalued by the predatory actions of others, a piece of the American Dream is stolen. Yes, there are corrupt politicians who support such behavior; however, eventually others will seek legislative solutions to protect the oppressed. Each generation of Americans has had to fight this battle. And with each emerging generation that seeks to hold onto the vision and ideals of the American Dream, we push back a little more of the darkness and are drawn into the light.

The great debate over the role of government and its responsibility in securing the American Dream continues to be a source of struggle today. The government is only needed to make and enforce laws that protect the American Dream. But government "intervention" has led to over-regulation and the takeover of private enterprises, which untimely destroys the Dream because it fosters dependence on the Federal Government and not on the market and competition and hard work.

In my view, the government's role is to protect the rights of its citizens and protect the American Dream. Yes, that means there have to be rules and regulations to guard against abuse. What I do not believe government should be doing, however, is over-regulating to the point that it inhibits the rights of its citizens and starts to strangle people's freedom and ability to pursue their dream. While laws and regulations are extremely important, it is equally important that they be user-friendly and that they strengthen and support enterprise and growth. When these laws make it harder to create and maintain small businesses, that hinders the American Dream.

It is this driving pursuit of the American Dream that is the source of combustion for the American economy. The hard work and willingness to do more to get ahead, continues to keep everyone on their toes. We need to keep the spirit in America. We need this driving force. But, there must be a payout at the end of the labor. There must be a reward.

> WASHINGTON HAS TRIED AND FAILED TO SECURE OUR BORDERS. . . . IT IS TIME FOR A NEW MODEL.

The Current Immigration Crisis

There are two things I believe Congress must do to fix our current immigration crisis. First, stronger measures must be taken on all of our borders to stop the flow of illegal immigrants into our country. We should be able to do this with as little disruption and as much efficiency as possible, which is why states that lie along our nation's borders should have more control over their own boundaries. As is evidenced in our current immigration problems, Washington has tried and failed to secure our borders in particular. It is time for a new model— the federal government should coordinate day-to-day state-led operations. After all, who is better primed to deal with the on-the-ground realities of porous boundaries?

Second, we must simplify the legalization process for legal immigrants. It currently takes almost a decade to become a citizen of the United States, including years of paperwork and other hurdles to obtain basic authorizations like working visas and green cards. But if we were to speed up the process, while at the same time maintaining practical standards, then all those who pass background checks and have no criminal records or infectious diseases should be given a two-year trial work visa. This trial period would enable them to work legally, which is the primary goal of immigration in the first place. This trial would also help to motivate them to maintain proper citizenship by paying taxes and working for the advancement of America. If at the end of this trial period the immigrants have met these standards, they should be allowed to apply for citizenship through a streamlined process.

The U.S. has much to offer—and much to receive. We can only reindustrialize if we allow hard-working immigrants to contribute and help rebuild our great nation. Especially in the fields of math and science, our international competitors have outpaced us. Indian engineers and Chinese software developers see the reality of the American Dream and want to come to this country with their expertise. But we need to give those who want to come here legally a fighting chance, by curtailing illegal immigration, streamlining the process to citizenship, and facilitating their study of our language, laws, and civic responsibilities.

CHAPTER 6

THE ENTREPRENEURIAL SPIRIT

"We all have dreams. But in order to make dreams come into reality, it takes an awful lot of determination, dedication, self-discipline, and effort."

—JESSE OWENS

Americans have always prided themselves on being uncompromising entrepreneurs. Economic fulfillment of the American Dream didn't commence with a large corporation. Instead, it sprouted from countless individuals and families starting small businesses and growing them. I am becoming more and more concerned that the combination of over-regulation, government intervention, and the unchecked greed and corruption among our government leaders is beginning to destroy the entrepreneurial spirit in our nation, a crucial part of the American Dream.

Every great success story in the annals of American business lore began with the creation of a small business. No company—not Merrill Lynch, General Electric, IBM, Microsoft, eBay, or any other you can think of—started as a large business or conglomerate. They began with one individual or a small handful of people with a good idea, invention, or service that they wanted to pursue—with ownership. Even today, approximately 75% of America's gross national product comes as the direct result of small business enterprise.

> EVERY PERSON WHO DREAMS OF OWNING THEIR OWN BUSINESS AND WHO IS WILLING TO WORK HARD . . . HAS THE RIGHT TO PURSUE THEIR DREAM.

The term "small business" is part and parcel with the American Dream. By that I mean this: every person who dreams of owning their own business and who is willing to work hard and sacrifice in order to make that business happen has the right to pursue their dream. Not only do they have the right to pursue it, but whatever success they achieve in turn allows them to employ others who themselves will benefit greatly. The American Dream is the small business owner's mantra.

Little Business, Big Success

My views on the value of small businesses and the role government should play in regulating them really stems from my childhood. My mother provided for our family for many years in large part by running a small business—a beauty salon she started in our home. She didn't take a government handout. Instead, she took out a loan from the Small Business Administration (SBA).

The SBA was established in 1953 when Congress passed the Small Business Act, which established a business development program to help small, disadvantaged businesses compete in the American economy and access the federal procurement market. The mission of the Small Business Administration is "to maintain and strengthen the nation's economy by enabling the establishment and viability of small businesses and by assisting in the economic recovery of communities after disasters." The SBA does not make loans directly to small businesses, but does help to educate and prepare the business owner to apply for a loan through a financial institution or bank. The SBA then acts as a guarantor on the bank loan.[3]

I remember watching my mother run and grow her business. I came to learn how she not only was able to benefit my family, she also benefited several other families as well. My mother often interacted with other merchants in the area; there were various vendors who depended on her business, and there were people who frequented her business. Her business was a living organism that impacted many others in our community.

Another good example from my own backyard in Harlem, is the true story of a local street vendor who put his three children through college by selling T-shirts, hats, and socks on the street. He did it legally; he did it ethically; he did it with a business license; he did it himself. Over a number of years, this entrepreneur gained the reputation and the know-how to be able to successfully launch others in that same business.

My wife is originally from Cape Verde, a group of islands 90 miles off the western coast of African Senegal. From the earliest days of the European slave trade, Cape Verde was the last stop before ships headed for Europe or the Americas from 1523 to 1832. A Portuguese colony until 1975, Cape Verde was one of the last countries in Africa to win independence.

Through the combination of necessity and ready opportunity, Cape Verdeans became great sailors, many of whom came to the United States and settled in the Massachusetts area, particularly around Hyannis Port and Martha's Vineyard. Slaves in their homeland, they found the freedom in the

United States to pursue business interests related to their sailing skills and achieve their particular American Dream.

These are just a few of the millions of similar stories about those who have achieved the American Dream through hard work and perseverance. New York City's rise to prominence was the result of immigrants from many diverse ethnic groups coming to America and using the skills they brought with them, fulfilling their American Dream. The great thing about the American Dream is that it is colorless, has no bounds, is indifferent to religious beliefs and, historically, has been available to every American.

> THE AMERICAN DREAM IS COLORLESS, HAS NO BOUNDS, IS INDIFFERENT TO RELIGIOUS BELIEFS AND, HISTORICALLY, HAS BEEN AVAILABLE TO EVERY AMERICAN.

The Value of Honor

Unfortunately, I fear that as a nation we are losing our grasp on this all-important ideal, not because we remain in the midst of one of the longest and deepest recessions this nation has seen, but because of excessive government and the bad examples of our leaders. There is always an intrinsic value to honesty and integrity.

Most of our democratic ideals rest on the principle of honor. Even our tax code is built on an honor system of sorts.

While the system is not perfect, it is still founded on the assumption that people are basically honest. But Wall Street, while always being aggressive, became greedy. This greed was left unchecked by the government, and it has eroded the American Dream. And that same greed amongst some of our politicians causes disillusionment, especially in the current economic environment.

Take for example, the great AIG and bank bailouts of 2009. Without even delving into the causes of the crisis, what happened to the money that the government loaned to big banks, mortgage companies, and brokerage firms? Did they use their bailouts to increase lending to businesses to help them recover? No. Did they write down mortgage and loan balances to help private citizens? No. Then, what did they do with the money? Well, it didn't find its way to existing small businesses or new entrepreneurs, that's for sure.

Then let's add to this the poison of excessive regulation, which circumvents a person's right to do business, and we start to destroy people's belief that they can fulfill the American Dream. Increasing regulation and bureaucracy are making it harder and harder for small businesses to survive as they fight their way through the process of governmental rules and red tape in order to be able to establish their "pushcart."

Governmental bureaucracy and red tape costs time and money, and the taxpayers pay the bill. For example, doctors that want to establish their own health clinics to practice family medicine in their communities face mountains of regulations, which ends up costing valuable time and money, which in turn raises the overall cost of healthcare. Regulations are of course important to protect individuals and prevent abuse. However, when carried to excess, or as is commonly the case—if the government regulation has little or nothing to with the process it is intended to regulate, it only restricts, chokes, and kills the entrepreneurial spirit.

A Plan for Change

As Americans, we have to promote, preserve, protect, and defend these dreams for the generations to come. How do we do that? Especially in Harlem and other inner cities, we have to clear the way for the creation of small businesses and we have to enable them to flourish once they are operational.

If elected, I will focus on limiting the current trend toward excessive government that inhibits the fulfillment of the American Dream through entrepreneurialism. To help me with this, I will sit down with real entrepreneurs in our community and have honest conversations about what needs to be done to reduce excessive regulation. I will do this not just so that I can lead effectively, armed with the experiences of my constituents, but also to start to rebuild community activism. Further, it is my desire to gather entrepreneurs together to seek ways to work together to benefit each other and our communities—just as immigrants in New York City have done for generations.

I will also work to promote microfinance in order to help revitalize our communities and cities. Currently, in many third world countries, missionaries and other international aid organizations are working to promote economic development through the concept of microfinance—the provision of common financial services to low-income clients, including consumers and the self-employed. Sometimes this simply involves a small loan that allows an individual or family to establish their own sustainable business. In other situations, it would provide access to high quality financial services, such as credit, savings, and insurance, to those who would not typically qualify. This movement has much potential to aid poor people in escaping poverty, as it would provide them with the opportunity to work hard in pursuit of the American Dream.

It is amazing to see the looks on people's faces when I tell them I am running for office and what I plan to do when elected. They believe it because they still have a part of the American Dream. Restoring what has been lost and what hinders that dream is the most important job any American can have right now.

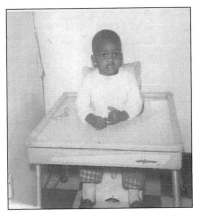

1959 Michel in high chair (2 years old)

1972 Sophomore year

1973 D.C. City Champs, Bishop McNamara High School (11 -0)

★ ★ ★

1973 Starting Defensive Tackle

1978 Virginia Tech Picture Day

1979 Virginia Tech photo day (Senior Year)

1981 NY Jets vs Atlanta Falcons (Pre-Season) (left to right)
Buddy Curry, Kenny Lewis, Mickey Fitzgerald, Michel Faulkner

1986 (Michel Faulkner, Dr. John Perkins, Dr. Jerry Falwell

1987 Lynchburg Virginia; Urban Ministry Conference; (left to right)
Michel Faulkner VP for Urban Ministry, Rev. Tom Maharris,
Dr. Sam Hines, Mr. Bill Sykes

★ ★ ★

Michel Faulkner

1999

*2003 Martin Luther King Jr. Awards program at Central Baptist Church
(Right to Left) Stanley Crouch (Columnist), Senator Chuck Schumer,
City Council Woman Gail Brewer*

★ ★ ★

2003 City Council Women Gail Brewer (good friend)

2003 Fund Raiser at Michael Bloomberg's home
(State Senator Joe Bruno, MF, Mayor Bloomberg

★ ★ ★

2003 Michel and Rudy

GEORGE E. PATAKI
GOVERNOR

June 7, 2003

Dear Reverend Faulkner:

It is a pleasure to send greetings and warm regards to you on the occasion of your *10th Anniversary* as Pastor of Central Baptist Church.

The Empire State proudly recognizes the men and women within the religious community who enrich the spiritual lives of its citizens. With unwavering resolve to your pastoral duties, you have built a solid foundation of faith and hope for the congregation of the Central Baptist Church. In leading by example, your effective ministry has encouraged strong, faith-based lifestyles where fellowship, respect, and service to others are held in high regard.

Today, you are honored by friends from throughout the community, and I join them in grateful appreciation for your charitable works and the significant impact they have on the parishioners of the Central Baptist Church as well as the many people living in the surrounding neighborhoods. Your leadership and religious stewardship is a special gift that promises to continue contributing in meaningful ways toward the betterment of society as a whole.

With my congratulations and best wishes for a memorable afternoon.

Very truly yours,

Reverend Michel J. Faulkner
Central Baptist Church
166 West 92nd Street
New York, NY 10025

2003 10th Anniversary Celebration Central Baptist Church

★ ★ ★

Mayor Michael R. Bloomberg Speaks at A Tribute to Martin Luther King Jr.
Central Baptist Church, Manhattan
January 18, 2004

all the best. Michael R Bloomberg

2004 Martin Luther King Jr. Awards program at Central Baptist Church:
Pastor Michel Faulkner; Mayor Michael Bloomberg

★ ★ ★

2006 Pastor Lee Rouson (Former NY Giant) Pastor Michel Faulkner
(Co-Pastors New Horizon Church)

2010 New York State Republican Convention

★ ★ ★

2010 Michel on Stage (Israel Day Rally in Central Park)

Michel with NY Jets Owner Woody Johnson (2010)

★ ★ ★

Running for Change

Wedding for Regis and Kelly

CHAPTER 7

RELIGION AND THE RULE OF LAW

"Freedom prospers when religion is vibrant and
the rule of law under God is acknowledged."

—RONALD REAGAN

The freedom to worship as one sees fit is inextricably bound to obtaining, living, and passing on the American Dream. For no matter what we believe about God, or whatever relationship we have with Him, the right to worship—or not—in the way we choose must be protected.

We often hear of the expression, "the separation of church and state." This statement has become such a common catch-phrase in our modern vernacular that most Americans believe it is a foundational principle of the Constitution, or included in the First Amendment. But in fact, this statement does not appear *anywhere* in the Constitution or the Declaration of Independence, or for that matter in any of our country's founding documents.

Rather, this phrase comes from a letter written by Thomas Jefferson to the Danbury Baptist Association stressing the importance of protecting the Church *from* government intervention and control. He was also reiterating the founding fathers' determination to prevent the establishment of a government-run religion or church. Jefferson's intent as one of the founders of our country was to establish freedom *of* religion, not freedom *from* religion.

One Nation under God

In an earlier chapter, I shared with you a quote from John Adams, second President of the United States, in which he said, "Our Constitution was made only for a moral and religious people. It is wholly inadequate to the government of any other." This means that our Constitution and Declaration of Independence require the moral assent of everyone that is governed; and I believe, by extension, by those we send to lead us in government.

This concept requires a fundamental understanding and acceptance that above man, there is God. Our nation and all that we have done has been predicated on the principle that God is the ultimate arbiter of justice. William Penn, an early champion of democracy and religious freedom, once said, "Men must be governed by God or they will be ruled by tyrants."

> "MEN MUST BE GOVERNED BY GOD OR THEY WILL BE RULED BY TYRANTS."
> —WILLIAM PENN

Freedom of religion is considered by many people to be a fundamental human right. Thomas Jefferson once said, "Among the inestimable of our blessings, also, is that . . . of liberty to worship our Creator in the way we think most agreeable to His will." We cannot have true liberty without religious freedom. But, we also cannot value the liberties that we enjoy without a common belief that these rights and privileges are endowed by our Creator.

Most of the immigrants coming to America were seeking religious freedom as well as economic prosperity. After they achieved it, the Declaration of Independence, and subsequently, the Constitution, protected those rights. ". . . We hold these things to be self evident, that all men are created equal and are endowed by their Creator with inalienable rights to life, liberty, and the pursuit of happiness." These inalienable rights endowed by our Creator are the founding principles upon which the American Dream is built; it is a desire that God has put into the hearts and minds of men and women who would seek him. Therefore, the American Dream and religious freedom are inseparable.

Establishing Freedom of Religion

Many of the early colonies were founded, in part, as a result of religious persecution within the colonies themselves. For instance, Roger Williams founded a new colony in Rhode Island to escape persecution in the theocratically-dominated colony of Massachusetts. Freedom of religion was first applied as a principle of government in the founding of the colony of Maryland. The Maryland Toleration Act, drafted by Lord Baltimore, is cited by *The Forum* at the Online Library of Liberty as being "the broadest definition of religious freedom during the seventeenth century and was an important step toward true freedom of religion."[4]

Reiterating Maryland's earlier colonial legislation, the Virginia Statute for Religious Freedom, written in 1779 by Thomas Jefferson, proclaimed, "[No] man shall be compelled to frequent or support any religious worship, place, or ministry whatsoever, nor shall be enforced, restrained, molested, or burdened in his body or goods, nor shall otherwise suffer, on account of his religious opinions or belief; but that all men shall be free to profess, and by argument to maintain, their opinions in matters of religion, and that the same shall in no wise diminish, enlarge, or affect their civil capacities."

I believe the doctrine of religious freedom actually flows from the doctrine of free will. So while I choose to serve God based on my Christian beliefs, I also believe that every man has the free will to deny God and that right has to be guaranteed and protected by government. God does not want coerced worship. The Bible says that God seeks those who will worship Him in spirit and in truth, (John 4:23). But I cannot worship God in spirit and in truth without free will. My role as a citizen of the United States calls me to protect the religious freedom of every citizen, regardless of whether we share the same views about religion.

A Conflict in the City

We are currently embroiled in a national debate stemming from the desire of several Islamic groups to build or establish an Islamic cultural center very close to the sites of the former World Trade Center buildings. The following is my recent public statement with regard to the proposed project.

Statement for Proposed Mosque Site
June 11, 2010

Today, I lend my voice to the growing number of voices expressing outrage and concern over the issues related to terrorist activities attached to religious beliefs and expressions. Religious terrorism is not new to America. We must remember that in the South just after the Civil War, newly freed African-American slaves were terrorized by so-called Christians wearing white robes. They operated with impunity for many years. Their views and acts of intimidation and terrorism in the name of religion had nothing to do with authentic Christianity. Rather they were cowards hiding their fear and hatred in the name of Jesus Christ.

The world we live in today is different, yet is much the same. There are terrorists living in America that will use the religion of Islam to hide their intentions to undermine or overthrow America. They must be stopped. I believe that there also are Muslims living in this country who are faithful to the religion of Islam and that do not want to see America overthrown or become an Islamic state. In every religion, there are extremists we cannot allow to operate with impunity for any reason.

This has been a very difficult issue for me to weigh in on because I believe fervently in religious freedom. The constitution states, "Congress shall make no law respecting an establishment of religion, or prohibiting the free exercise thereof." But Ground Zero is a sacred burial ground; this site is where terrorist activities claimed the lives of more than 3000 innocent people.

This site is not an appropriate location to house a mosque. To build a mosque at this location would infringe on the rights and memories of others, because this site marks the resting place of thousands who lost their lives as a result of terrorist activities and hatred.

Muslims should be free to build mosques and to have expressions of their religion wherever they choose, provided that they do not infringe upon the rights of others. I think it is inappropriate to have a mosque on this site. If it is simply a matter of building a mosque or an Islamic cultural center, that can be done anywhere and does not have to be at the center of the location where thousands lost their lives at the hands of Islamic terrorists hiding behind the religion of Islam.

I call upon peace-loving, freedom-loving Muslims to join us in this struggle and lend your voice to dissuade the leaders of this movement from continuing their quest to erect a cultural center on this location.

In a country where numerous and distinct ethnic, religious, and cultural groups are present and tolerated, there are bound to be encroachments on the customs of others. What has made America great is the respect and commitment that we have made to allow others to worship God as they please. This is, of course, predicated upon the assumption that no one should ever be forced to worship or coerced into worshiping or bowing to any deity against their will.

As a Baptist minister, this is one of the fundamental theological propositions upon which my faith is built. While I do not agree with all religions and religious expressions, I have and will defend their right to exercise their freedom as vigorously as I will defend my right to exercise that freedom.

A Threat to Liberty

The issue of Muslim law being propagated throughout America—even as is currently happening in Europe—threatens to steal the American Dream. Sharia law based on the Koran says that all people in a region should be governed by the Islamic law; that they should be offered an opportunity to submit willingly to that law, and that if they refuse, they should be forced into obeying the Islamic law. This belief flies in the face of the Constitution and the American Dream.

Specifically, the idea or notion that anyone would be forced or coerced to worship in a form or fashion that they did not agree with because of legal or cultural dictates is offensive. It is offensive to the founding principles of this nation and it poses the greatest threat to religious freedom that we have ever seen in our country. We desire to celebrate our personal liberties and to extend the same freedoms to all who come to the United States. However, when those who enjoy the liberties America offers would use their influence to encroach upon the freedoms of others, that represents a clear violation of the freedoms and liberties guaranteed in the Constitution and the Declaration of Independence.

We have allowed the notion of political correctness to take us down a dark road in which the light of reason, wisdom, and common sense no longer shine. In a time of increasing tension and conflict, we need to understand and remember that the dream makes freedom possible for everyone and not just for a chosen few.

> ★ WE HAVE
> ★ ALLOWED THE
>   NOTION OF
> ★ POLITICAL
> ★ CORRECTNESS
>   TO TAKE US
> ★ DOWN A DARK
> ★ ROAD IN WHICH
>   THE LIGHT OF
> ★ REASON,
> ★ WISDOM, AND
>   COMMON SENSE
> ★ NO LONGER
> ★ SHINE.

My beliefs as an evangelical Christian minister call me to invite others to know of my God and how they can have a personal relationship with Him through Jesus Christ. However, this is in no way an invitation or justification for me to encroach upon the personal freedoms of others, demanding they attend or submit to religious indoctrination by me or any other Christian minister. I would oppose these tactics as vigorously as I now oppose the Muslim fundamentalist tactics to impose Sharia law on America. While my faith is personal and I do seek to share it with others, it must be received willingly and voluntarily by all who would choose to hear it.

RESTORING THE AMERICAN DREAM
★ ★ ★

If the American Dream is going to be kept alive in order to be passed on to the next generation, we must have true freedom of religion.

★ ★ ★

CHAPTER 8

A LIGHT ON THE HILL

"In the political sense, there is one problem that currently underlies all of the others. That problem is making government sufficiently responsive to the people. If we don't make government responsive to the people, we don't make it believable. And we must make government believable if we are to have a functioning democracy."

—PRESIDENT GERALD R. FORD

Each of the three branches of our government has responsibilities uniquely different from the others. The legislative branch (led by the two houses of Congress) makes the laws.

The executive branch (led by the President) enforces the laws. The judicial branch (headed by the Supreme Court) interprets the laws. And, if you follow politics at all, you know that it's actually much more complicated than that.

For example, while Congress does make the laws, the President is responsible for ratifying the laws written by Congress. And, should the President reject a new law, Congress can override the President. As another example, while the courts interpret the laws, many judges are appointed by the President, such as our Supreme Court justices; however, those appointments must first be confirmed by Congress. And, to make matters even more complicated, all of our fifty states have rights, some of which supersede national regulation and some of which do not.

OUR FOUNDING FATHERS SET UP OUR GOVERNMENT WITH SO MANY CHECKS AND BALANCES TO PROTECT US FROM OURSELVES AND FROM THE ABUSE OF POWER.

If you don't believe me, follow the ins and outs of the recent battle between the State of Arizona and the Federal Government over Arizona's immigration law. Or, follow some of the recent legal challenges filed by some states against President Obama's recently passed healthcare legislation. There is a reason why our founding fathers set up our government with so many checks and balances—to protect us from ourselves and from the abuse of power.

But there is another critical component to our government, and that is: *we the people.* Our democracy requires that the majority of Americans pay attention and believe in the integrity of the system. The security of our freedom requires that we ask questions and educate ourselves on the issues; that we vote and demand accountability of our elected officials. Without our active participation, the rule of law is not taken seriously and therefore every law that is passed is taken with a grain of salt. When Americans become mistrusting and apathetic about democracy, democracy does not work. If we lose faith in our leaders and our government, we lose our grip on the American Dream.

Fighting for our Future

As modern Americans, we have allowed our political system to operate in ways that do not work in the best interests of democracy. In the name of the laws and liberties that we have come to honor and revere, we have allowed today's politicians to take our country to the brink of destruction. We must now return to a common moral agenda—one in which each individual is held accountable for their deeds—to truly promote the ideals encompassed by the expression "liberty and justice for all."

Ronald Reagan once said, "Freedom is never more than one generation away from extinction. We didn't pass it to our children in the bloodstream. It must be fought for, protected, and handed on for them to do the same." This truth is not a modern concept; in fact it can be traced back through the annals of recorded history.

In the Old Testament of the Bible, each time a promise was given to one of the patriarchs of Israel, he had to fight to secure that promise in his generation and in order to preserve the continued blessing for future generations. The Jewish Law and worldview was to be passed from one generation to the next. Each patriarch had to instill those values in his children and teach them to instill it in their children, and so on. This Judeo-Christian principle of generational inspiration must continue to be one of our fundamental promises and beliefs as it relates to our democratic form of government.

Deep in the heart of every American there is a longing for freedom and liberty and justice. That is part of the American Dream. But in order to have the promise of the American Dream, we must elect citizens that understand and believe in this concept. These values are not selfish or altruistic but rather egalitarian and selfless. Our problem has been that selfless values have given way to greed and corruption and moral failures on the part the men and women we have elected to serve our interest. It seems that we can't totally drain the swamp unless we have a movement of Americans who are willing to stand up and talk about what citizenship is and how it is important to the future of America and the American Dream.

For the People

"Democracy is the government of the people,
by the people, for the people."

— ABRAHAM LINCOLN

As those we elected to serve on our behalf earned our mistrust, the American people began to doubt not only the politicians but also the system itself. Remember, the United States is a republic that is based on a representative government in which we don't elect leaders, we elect representatives to serve on our behalf. In our form of democracy, we have established the good faith belief that the people's voice is the voice that our politicians will serve. Since it is impossible for a everyone to show up at "government" to make decisions, laws, and the like, we have representatives that we trust to represent what is in the best interest of all the people.

> TO SERVE ON OUR BEHALF AND REPRESENT US, OUR ELECTED REPRESENTATIVES MUST BE MORAL AND ETHICAL.

To serve on our behalf and represent us, our elected representatives must be moral and ethical. When we discover that elected officials are not moral, how can we trust that they represent their constituencies rather than representing their own personal interests? When our leaders are not moral, they need to be sanctioned or removed from office in order to protect both the citizens and trust in our government. Greed and corruption undermine the basic fabric of our nation's security and has to be dealt with. The book of Proverbs makes this point repeatedly with passages like these:

"When the righteous prosper, the city rejoices; when the wicked perish, there are shouts of joy," (Proverbs 11:10 NIV).

"When the wicked rise to power, people go into hiding; but when the wicked perish, the righteous thrive," (Proverbs 28:28 NIV).

"When the righteous thrive, the people rejoice; when the wicked rule, the people groan," (Proverbs 29:2 NIV).

When our representatives don't represent the highest moral order, then they undermine the fabric of our government and mock the very flag and Constitution that they swore to protect. We must be willing to remove them; that we can restore the American Dream for the next generation.

We must have the courage to hold our elected representatives to a higher moral standard—the moral standard necessary to be a good citizen, not just a crafty, slick politician. If the moral character of our elected representatives is lacking, then we separate each American from the decisions that these representatives reach. The separation is created by a growing distrust and dissatisfaction because we don't believe that decisions are being made in the people's best interest.

We are beginning to see a dramatic increase in government involvement, regulation, and control of American life. Our government clearly has a role in protecting its people; however, America also was founded on the precept that people should be free to pursue their American Dream without excessive regulation. The regulation of free markets has to find its balance and trust and faith in our common moral fabric. Regulation to protect against excess if fine; however regulation should be based on what is in the best interests of the people—not in what is in the best interest of growing government or increasing its control. Problems occur when government begins to speak for its own self-interest, control, and power, as opposed to the best interests of the people.

Our government's role with regard to regulation should be to preserve, protect, and defend the freedoms and liberties of our nation by making and enforcing laws that preserve and protect those freedoms. The government goes off track when it begins to make laws that elevate government and government leaders above the law.

> ★ THE GOVERNMENT GOES OFF TRACK WHEN IT BEGINS TO MAKE LAWS THAT ELEVATE GOVERNMENT AND GOVERNMENT LEADERS ABOVE THE LAW.

A Failure of Duty

In recent months our elected representatives have failed greatly in representing the best interests of the people. A significant example is the recent healthcare bill that was signed into law. Shockingly, most of those elected officials signed the law and committed the American people to a plan they did not fully understand. Although there was great debate at the time of the vote on the bill, the bill was not complete—it was left unfinished with "fill-in-the-blanks" to be inserted later. The details were unfinished and yet despite that fact, it was still signed into law. We may spend the next 10 years sorting through the details of this bill and trying to eradicate the tentacles of government takeover from our healthcare system.

Another very pointed example of the failures of our current congressional leadership was the confirmation of Secretary Geithner as Secretary of the Treasury. While Mr. Geithner's qualifications are certainly impressive, there was one glaring disqualification that seemed to be completely overlooked by those who confirmed his appointment: Mr. Geithner did not pay personal income taxes for four years. It was also disclosed that the company he worked for had actually written him a check designated for his taxes and required him to sign a document verifying that he used that money to pay those taxes that he, in fact, did not pay. In my opinion, this is a non-negotiable disqualification for the office that he holds. We can't trust him because he didn't pay his taxes and to have him occupy this position separates us as common citizens from influencing the decisions that he makes.

The Big Lie of Big Government

As the government continues to grow larger and take more control over the lives of common citizens, we sacrifice liberty for what the government promises to do. Thomas Jefferson said, "a government that is big enough to give you whatever you want is strong enough to take whatever you have." I believe we face a greater threat in this generation because the government has been infringing upon the liberties of people and the free markets.

Most Americans don't understand the real need and value of a free-market economy. What our government is essentially saying is that the market can no longer take care of people and provide for them in accordance with what they need. So, therefore, we need government regulations and regulatory agencies that need to be created in order to protect the interests of the people. I disagree with this trend because I believe it diminishes the creativity, freedom, and liberty that are the hallmarks of the ingenuity of the American people.

During the Great Depression of the 1930s, there was a church in Harlem by the name of Abyssinian Baptist Church that fed the community and provided resources and assistance without any government programs or financing. At the same time, this church maintained a balanced budget and paid off the mortgage on its building using the tithes and offerings of its members. This church's pastor was Adam Clayton Powell,

Sr., the father of the first congressman from this district, Adam Clayton Powell, Jr.

The idea that we need government to "solve our problems" is a completely un-American idea. This concept is called "Big Government." While many still laud Roosevelt's New Deal as the impetus for our recovery from the Great Depression, the reality is that it was not. While Roosevelt's New Deal did resolve some immediate problems, the Great Depression didn't really end until we started cranking up the U.S. economy to prepare for and supply the American military during World War II. Further, the New Deal paved the way for increased government control and tampering with the markets.

Government dependency weakens our nation. It stifles the creativity and individuality that our nation was founded upon. Can you imagine if we had a regulatory agency that controlled the westward expansion in the 1800s? What we continue to struggle with is the balance between creativity and the rule of law. We must find that balance and maintain it in order to ensure that there is an American Dream to pass on to the next generation.

Time for A Revolution

"You can never have a revolution in order to establish a democracy. You must have a democracy in order to have a revolution."

—GILBERT K. CHESTERTON

Forty years ago our nation launched a "war on poverty." This war was due in no small part to white guilt over years of slavery and racial discrimination against black Americans. While President Johnson's Great Society was good on some levels, it also created dependency rather than promoting self-sufficiency. Ultimately, in some ways this initiative crippled the black community and started a trend toward multi-generational poverty. Throughout the 1980s, the inner city—and the black family—continued to unravel. Child poverty stayed close to 20 percent, hitting a high of 22.7 percent in 1993. Welfare dependency continued to rise, soaring from two million families in 1970 to five million by 1995. By 1990, 65 percent of all black children were being born to unmarried women.

In black communities like Central Harlem, the number was closer to 80 percent. By this point, no one doubted that most of these children were destined to grow up poor and pass down the legacy of single parenting to their own children.[5]

Now, more than $3 trillion of government support later, we have come to conclude that government intervention to resolve social malaise is ineffective at best and most likely detrimental to the community it attempts to help. The American Dream always has

THE AMERICAN DREAM ALWAYS HAS BEEN BUILT ON THE COMBINATION SELF-DETERMINATION AND OPPORTUNITY.

been built on the combination self-determination and opportunity. This Dream cannot be sustained into the next generation through spoon-feeding or coddling. Each generation must pay its dues in order to reap the desired reward. When our government decides that it knows what is best and begins to engineer outcomes, particularly for the poor or voiceless, there are major problems.

Right now we have a desperate need in our nation for a re-visitation of the self-determination speeches of Dr. Martin Luther King, Booker T. Washington, and even Malcolm X. What these pioneers understood and our government has failed to grasp is that the changes can only be made by individuals and not through government edicts. We must remain committed to the idea and the notion that we will reap what we sow; and we must demand that government preserve, protect, and defend the rights and liberties of each American.

In the preservation of these rights and liberties, we must insist that our government level the playing field, ensuring that everyone has an equal opportunity. Because of the recent negative trends in our country, it will take some time to close the gap of despair. It is not too late to restore the American Dream for this generation. But we must begin now. We don't have another day or another generation to waste.

CHAPTER 9

★ ★ ★

THE COST OF COMPROMISE

"Now, I say to you today my friends, even though we face the difficulties of today and tomorrow, I still have a dream. It is a dream deeply rooted in the American dream. I have a dream that one day this nation will rise up and live out the true meaning of its creed: 'We hold these truths to be self-evident, that all men are created equal.'"

—MARTIN LUTHER KING, JR.

Since America's inception, our leaders have struggled with the inevitable battle between their conscience and the fruits of power. But one conflict in particular—the struggle with race—has plagued every generation since the founding of this great nation. First through the oppression of slavery and then during the fight for racial equality in the post-Civil War era, racial bigotry has stifled the American Dream for many. "Slavery was no side show in American history—it was the main event," said historian James Horton.

We have held the founders of this nation in such high regard that we often forget that they were flawed human beings just as we are. Until the Civil War, our nation and its leaders struggled with the implications and consequences of years of compromise in regard to slavery. Leaders often found themselves trying to reconcile themselves to policies with respect to slavery that were contrary to their understanding of the fundamental principles of the American Dream.

While many were personally and fundamentally opposed to slavery, they also understood that, in many ways, slavery helped fuel the economic engine that supported our free-market economy. Yet, for all their flaws, our founding fathers did sign into law the Declaration of Independence and the Constitution of the United States. It is imperative that we wrestle with their conflict in order to learn from them, as the compromise that nearly destroyed the American Dream is still among us.

THE COST OF COMPROMISE
★ ★ ★

A Contradiction of Conviction

If you consider the history of our country, it might astonish you to realize that America was a slave country for much longer than it has been a free one. The first slaves arrived on our shores in 1619, and it was 246 years before slavery was abolished by the passage of the 13th amendment in 1865. As a truly free country, from 1865 to 2010, America is only 145 years old.

There were very few men who were as influential in America's fight for independence and freedom as Thomas Jefferson. But he was no less conflicted about the compromise that divided north from south, friend from neighbor, and brother from brother. According to the Jefferson Encyclopedia:[6]

"Thomas Jefferson was a consistent opponent of slavery throughout his life. He considered it contrary to the laws of nature that decreed that everyone had a right to personal liberty. He called the institution an 'abominable crime' a 'moral depravity,' a 'hideous blot,' and a 'fatal stain' that deformed 'what nature had bestowed on us of her fairest gifts.'

"Early in his political career Jefferson took actions that he hoped would end in slavery's abolition. He drafted the Virginia law of 1778 prohibiting the importation of enslaved Africans. In 1784 he proposed an ordinance banning slavery in the new territories of the

Northwest. From the mid-1770s he advocated a plan of gradual emancipation, by which all born into slavery after a certain date would be declared free.

"As historian David Brion Davis noted, if Jefferson had died in 1785, he would be remembered as an anti-slavery hero, as 'one of the first statesmen anywhere to advocate concrete measures for eradicating slavery.'"

However, Jefferson's actions weren't always consistent with his words or beliefs. The Jefferson Encyclopedia continued in this regard to say:

"After that time, however, there came a 'thundering silence.' Jefferson made no public statements on American slavery nor did he take any significant public action to change the course of his state or his nation.

"Countless articles and even entire books have been written trying to explain the contradictions between Jefferson's words and actions in regard to slavery. His views on race, which he first broadcast in his Notes on the State of Virginia in 1785, unquestionably affected his behavior. His belief in the inferiority of blacks, coupled with their presumed resentment of their former owners, made their removal from the United States an integral part of Jefferson's emancipation scheme. These convictions were exacerbated by the bloody revolution in Haiti and an aborted rebellion of slaves and free blacks in Virginia in 1800.

"While slavery remained the law of the land, Jefferson struggled to make ownership of humans compatible with the new ideas of the era of revolutions. By creating a moral and social distance between himself and enslaved people, by pushing them down the "scale of beings," he could consider himself as the "father" of "children" who needed his protection.

"As he wrote of slaves in 1814, 'brought up from their infancy without necessity for thought or forecast, [they] are by their habits rendered as incapable as children of taking care of themselves.' In the manner of other paternalistic slaveholders, he thus saw himself as the benevolent steward of the African Americans to whom he was bound in a relation of mutual dependency and obligation.

"By 1820, during the political crisis that resulted in the Missouri Compromise, Jefferson had come to believe that the spread of slavery into the west—its 'diffusion'—would prove beneficial to the slaves and hasten the end of the institution. The prospect of a geographical line based on principle running across the country, 'like a fire bell in the night, awakened and filled me with terror.' He feared it could threaten the union and lead to civil war.

"As always, his primary concern was the stability of the nation he had helped to found. Almost forty years after Jefferson's death, slavery was ended by the bloodiest war in American history."

A Foreshadow of Change

Like many of his contemporaries, George Washington was also deeply troubled by slavery. Unlike most, however, Washington actually acted upon his convictions. It is unfortunate that Washington did not abolish slavery during his presidency, and we can only wish he had done more. But he did choose to do four important things.

First, during the American Revolution, Washington accepted blacks, including recently emancipated slaves, into the Continental Army. Then at some point during the war, Washington determined that he would no longer buy and sell slaves. He did not waver from that decision.

Third, Washington used slaves as overseers and managers on his plantations. Perhaps because of his wartime experience, Washington knew that blacks were competent and they could do the same jobs as whites. In fact, Washington's farms were "revolutionary" in their commitment to treat blacks as if they were just like everyone else.

Finally, at the end of his life Washington did something to end slavery on a personal level—he emancipated all of his slaves in his will.

These lessons from history affirm the fact that while the two greatest architects of American freedom were indeed great men, they were still willing to compromise in their pursuit of the American Dream. I do not mention the flaws and struggles of Thomas Jefferson and George Washington for sensationalism or

THE VALUES AND IDEALS OF THE AMERICAN DREAM MUST CONSTANTLY BE PLACED ABOVE ALL OTHER CONSIDERATIONS.

exploitation; but merely as an illustration of the fact that the values and ideals of the American Dream must constantly be placed above all other considerations. If we are not faithful to uphold them, the consequences to our country will be no less devastating than the effects of the choices of our founding fathers in regards to slavery.

It is very important that we understand our responsibility to further the ideals of America in spite of the flaws or compromises of those who have gone before us. In many ways, their struggles are what make America great, for each generation has the opportunity to improve on the past. With history as our lens and God as our guide, we can only succeed by learning from the mistakes of the past and upholding the ideals of America and the American Dream.

Even today, our leaders need to do more than just stand by and allow amoral behavior to continue, especially if the perpetrators are leaders among them and such behavior interferes with the survival of the American Dream. What will our children think when they see and hear daily, through various mediums, that their heroes and leaders do not practice what they preach? Shouldn't we be a generation that models the right way to go and the right thing to do? In order to do that we must embrace the failures of the past and move boldly and with conviction toward an uncertain future armed with the American Dream and our commitment to restore it for the next generation.

CHAPTER 10

THE RACIAL DIVIDE

"Racism is a refuge for the ignorant. It seeks to divide and to destroy. It is the enemy of freedom, and deserves to be met head-on and stamped out."

—PIERRE BERTON

The compromise of slavery almost destroyed this nation. It is important for us to remember the political climate that led to the Civil War so that it will never happen again. The Civil War forced us as a nation to pay the price of compromise—and the cost was incalculable in terms of loss of life and future leaders. But we must recognize that the efforts to preserve the Union were also intended to protect the

WHILE SLAVERY NEARLY DESTROYED OUR COUNTRY, IT IS ALSO TRUE THAT THE INSTITUTION OF SLAVERY WAS FUNDAMENTAL IN BUILDING THIS NATION.

American Dream and to ensure its survival for all generations to come. Frankly, were it not for the underlying goal of preserving the American Dream, it is likely that many would not have fought and the Union ultimately would not have been preserved.

Yet, while the compromise of slavery nearly destroyed our country, it is also true that the institution of slavery was fundamental in building this nation. This contradiction demands that we reconcile it so that we may heal as a nation—especially since our founding fathers' belief in equal rights for all has still not been fully effected in our great, but flawed nation. The emancipation proclamation did not heal the wounds of slavery. We can only truly heal as a nation when we understand what caused this to occur in the first place and to never again allow such compromises to threaten or steal the American Dream.

The "Race Card"

Recent accusations against the Tea Party Movement as being controlled by racists has taken us all back a few years. You can always tell when a debate is getting heated when someone throws out the "race card." One of the positive results of

President Obama's election is that we have all been forced to examine our feelings and attitudes about race more honestly.

In this age of political correctness no one wants to be branded a racist. Liberals still hold the accusation of racism as a trump card to be played whenever things start getting out of their control. And when they make the accusation, it is seldom challenged.

Unfortunately the American public is addicted to sound bites. When most of us hear a sound bite we never bother to investigate the reliability or the context with which the statement is made—we simply assume it is true.

★ RACISM IS ONE
★ OF THOSE
BITTER AND
★ DIVIDING ISSUES
★ THAT WE
SELDOM FACE
★ WITH REASON.
★ OUR RESPONSE
IS USUALLY
★ EMOTIONAL,
★ WHICH MOST
OFTEN LEADS TO
★ THE WRONG
★ CONCLUSIONS.

And the race card is a more effective rallying point than most. Racism is one of those bitter and dividing issues that we seldom face with reason. Our response is usually emotional, which most often leads to the wrong conclusions.

Webster's Dictionary defines racism as, "A belief that race is the primary determinant of human traits and capacities and that racial differences produce an inherent superiority of a particular race." The *Encyclopedia Britannica* elaborates on racism as being "any action, practice, or belief that reflects the racial worldview—the ideology that humans are divided into separate and exclusive biological entities called 'races,' that there is a causal link between inherited physical traits and traits of personality, intellect, morality, and other cultural behavioral features, and that some races are innately superior to others."

The consistent theme is that one who is racist believes and acts as if another person is superior or inferior to others by virtue of their race or ethnic background. The bottom line is that racism is a power issue. It grows from one human being's desire to oppress another and uses race as a method of exploiting differences. Racism has played a major part in the dysfunction of our nation since our inception. But each generation has had a champion or group of champions to remind us of what the Declaration of Independence and the Constitution really represent for all people.

Dr. Martin Luther King, Jr. and those who joined with him in the non-violent Civil Rights movement of the 1960s confronted dogs, fire hoses, and guns, armed only with their faith in God and the rule of law. They were the powerful champions of their generation and confronted America with the truth that it was not living up to its creed and ideals. This was a vivid illustration of the truly powerless confronting the powerful.

Civil Rights leaders challenged the white establishment's laws, ideas, institutions, and traditions on behalf of the powerless or the less powerful. This confrontation, as painful as it was to watch, resulted in unjust laws being changed, and forced America to examine its treatment of its citizens against the immutable standard of the founding ideals and documents of Liberty. Most people didn't want to be accused of being on the wrong side of that issue.

Bridging the Gap

But the racial divide in America is part of the fabric of our culture. It is what President Obama has called "America's original sin." We must all embrace that fact and agree on certain ground rules for dialog in the public square today.

> BUT THE RACIAL DIVIDE IN AMERICA IS PART OF THE FABRIC OF OUR CULTURE. IT IS WHAT PRESIDENT OBAMA HAS CALLED "AMERICA'S ORIGINAL SIN."

We most certainly will not always agree. White Americans need to understand that communities of color are still very sensitive about issues of racial discrimination. Because of our blood-stained past, those sensitivities must be addressed with respect if we are going to have a meaningful dialog to advance the cause of liberty for all. White Americans must also understand that the true champions for liberty and freedom must learn to speak the language of inclusion, because that is what the Constitution and the Declaration of Independence demands.

On the other hand, Americans of color—particularly the African-American community—must understand that the national sin of slavery is behind us. Our ancestors dreamed and longed for the day and time in which we live. And although the playing field is not yet completely level, we must understand that the remaining distance to be traveled must be navigated with an honest and sincere belief in the American Dream and the promises and ideals of our founding precepts, and is not necessarily dependent on the good wishes of all white Americans, but rather is part of the creed of America.

We must also realize that there are some prominent African-Americans that have made their living by fueling the fires of racial division. They have missed the true message of Dr. King and the Civil Rights Movement. The Civil Rights Movement was a battle for equal opportunities—not hand-outs or bailouts. Most of these leaders do not have the same agenda or dignity of Dr. King, yet they continue to trade on his memory and work for their own personal gain and not for the collective good of all people.

Finally, the African-American community must acknowledge that we have racist elements within our ranks as well. Those who believe that all white people are against them simply because they are black are controlled by the same racism that rules the white supremacist. These individuals are not looking for ways to advance true equality, but rather they seek opportunities to exploit white guilt. When the media promotes these voices as the spokespeople for all, or even a majority of black people, they do us all a great injustice.

If we are going to move forward we all must deal with race and the "race card" differently. We have to understand that is never any reason or cause that would make using racial epitaphs or signs acceptable. We must also realize that there are those that would accuse the Tea Party of being racist simply to attempt to discredit their demands for President Obama and this administration to change direction. It is our duty as American citizens to petition and challenge our government for redress and change. It is our duty to call attention to the destructive forces that are expanding our Federal Government to swell to unparalleled levels. We must demand these things of the President and of every elected official. We must also require that all of our representatives work for the collective good of all Americans—regardless of race.

CHAPTER 11

THE INFORMATION AGE

"Many a small thing has been made large by the right kind of advertising."

—MARK TWAIN

With the expansion of electronic mass media, it became possible for the American Dream to reach the common person with blazing speed. Liberty and justice are intrinsic values that are part of the internal belief system of America. It is, in a word, what we fundamentally believe about America. But our media and mass communications are essential tools that can either enhance or destroy the American Dream.

Electronic media gave the ideal of democracy a visual imagery, much like our flesh covers our skeletal structure to give shape to the body. Through these mediums, the American Dream has a picture attached to it. This picture may or may not be accurate; however, it is communicated to millions of people with an ever-increasing speed. These realities present challenges that must be addressed. When the reality of the perfect picture or visual image of the American Dream is not realized, we must be able to do an accurate assessment to find out where the discrepancy lies. Our pursuit must focus on truth and not on fantasy. Propaganda, both good and bad, has been a tool of government since the written word was established. Now, in the age of information—that propaganda, both good and bad, has a powerful visual imagery attached to it.

This was especially true immediately after World War II. The victorious soldiers returned home and the nation set out to enjoy the prosperity that would come with victory. We shared a common enemy in the Soviet Union and a common belief in the goodness of America. Those images of a "perfect" America became representations of the American Dream and were reinforced by every possible medium at the time. They were packaged and sold to Americans at great profit regardless of the truthfulness or the health of these images.

One example was found in the tobacco industry. Cigarette advertising deliberately projected a certain "image" and created a multibillion-dollar industry, despite the fact that tobacco manufacturers were aware of the detrimental effects of nicotine—an addictive, life-controlling substance found in every cigarette. Not only were the tobacco growers making a huge profit on their product, but they were also being subsidized by the federal government through various agricultural programs. The profitability of cigarette manufacturing and distribution was reinforced and assisted by television advertising and even television programs with images of successful people smoking.

Madison Avenue ad agencies began advertising their version of the American Dream and Americans began snapping it up. Carefully crafted and packaged, the "dream" was designed to appeal to the greatest cross section of people. While these images were not always accurate, they were certainly enticing. Thanks to the freedoms and liberties that we have come to enjoy, Americans were soon able to purchase the fantasy version of the American Dream if the real one was too austere.

> ★ THANKS TO THE FREEDOMS AND LIBERTIES THAT WE HAVE COME TO ENJOY, AMERICANS WERE SOON ABLE TO PURCHASE THE FANTASY VERSION OF THE AMERICAN DREAM IF THE REAL ONE WAS TOO AUSTERE.

Pictures Worth a Thousand Words

The news media during the 60s continued to be a very important part of preserving an accurate description of both what was wrong and right with America. Television news also forced us to look at war and the Civil Rights Movement in a new way. Television brought the imagery associated with Jim Crow segregation into every home. It connected a visual imagery of the American Dream and its reality. In this case, mass media forced us to examine the American Dream and answer the questions associated with years of compromise.

The images of our compromise were balanced by the entertainment industry that showed integration and equality among races as an achievable reality. Two examples of this were *Star Trek* and *I Spy*. Both of these programs had black actors playing leading roles alongside white actors. The images were strong and it gave the impression that integration was an achievable and seamless process. While, in reality, a full ten years after the Supreme Court decision disallowing "separate but equal" schools, our schools and many other places in the nation were still fully segregated.

While the entertainment industry balanced the reality of the racial divide, the line between news and entertainment began to blur. As we became dependent on electronic communications for up-to-date and accurate information, these agencies became more driven by ratings and profit through advertising than by the truth. As we became an increasingly entertainment-centered culture, entertainment became big business and big business began to dominate the news.

Yet again, in this generation we were faced with the question "does the end justify the means"? The media has been infected by the same corruption and greed that continues to try and rob us of the American Dream. For all the good that television and mass media have provided, it has also implanted some unhealthy and unrealistic fantasies in the hearts of Americans.

> ★ THE MEDIA HAS
> ★ BEEN INFECTED
> BY THE SAME
> ★ CORRUPTION
> ★ AND GREED
> THAT
> ★ CONTINUES
> ★ TO TRY AND
> ROB US OF THE
> ★ AMERICAN
> ★ DREAM.

Freedom of the Press?

The second amendment to the United States Constitution guarantees us freedom of religion and the freedom of speech and press. These liberties are at the core of the American Dream and once they are compromised, the reality of the Dream begins to ebb away. The free press, unencumbered by government intervention, was seen by our nation's founders as a tool and a resource for and by the people to inform the public and hold government accountable. Without a free and unbiased press, democracy cannot function.

We are especially vulnerable to attacks in this area in this day and age because of the rapid speed at which thoughts are communicated around the globe. With the invention of the Internet and its exponential development and social media networks, the volume of information that we share and the speed at which we disseminate and receive it is mind-boggling.

As a communications major in college, I learned that journalism and the American free press were built on the principles of accurately reporting the facts—unembellished and untainted by personal opinions or other biases. Of course, the rationale behind this principle was very simple. If people could hear an accurate unbiased description of what was being said and who was saying it, they could determine for themselves the relevance. The founders also understood that if the press were not free, then it would be used as a tool for coercion and control of the minds of the common citizen. Our democracy rests on a common belief that, when citizens make wise and informed choices, we help our government through full participation and accountability.

> THE FREE PRESS IS NO LONGER FREE—IT HAS BEEN BOUGHT AND SOLD.

I believe that is no longer true for mass media outlets because they are controlled by commercial and entertainment interests rather than by organizations dedicated to reporting the news. The free press is no longer free—it has been bought and sold. Thank God for the Internet. Free expression has found a communication medium through the Internet. However, the Internet has a great flaw: information travels without any review by a responsible editorial board. Any person can send images or post a blog and most of us that use the Internet as a source of information rely on the opinions of others—most of whom clearly have biased agendas.

A Digital Disconnect

In this age of instant information we don't read as much. We don't study the meta narratives (history, the Bible, and so on). We look at history as someone's opinion and not necessarily as truth. Most Americans don't know their rights as guaranteed by the constitution. Voting is down; community involvement is down. This doesn't mean that people don't care. The Internet opens up millions of micro-communities. We think we can phone in or text in our views, instead of joining with others in our community to "make something happen." Whatever you may think of the activist groups of the 1960s or today's Tea Party, I do credit them for joining together and speaking up for what they believed in and challenging what they thought was wrong.

This generation is in danger of losing the American Dream because of the global nature of our ability to travel and to do other things in other places. This tends to give one the illusion that taking care of things on the home front can be done somehow with an absentee ballot. We cannot phone in democracy. It has to be handled up close and personal. The late great Tip O'Neal said, "all politics is local." I would add to that, that democracy has to happen at the retail level.

Meaning, people have to be involved personally in the lives of others in their community to have the greatest impact. People have to get involved.

For example, during the Civil Rights Movement, the first major lunch counter boycotts were not coordinated. The first big coordinated event was the Montgomery bus boycott, which was started by Rosa Parks—unannounced, unplanned, and unrehearsed. The woman was tired. Every night for 374 days, people were gathered together in Montgomery, Alabama, in black churches to find out what was going on. There were no fax machines. There were no cell phones. There was no Internet. Communication was passed from pastor to pastor, from person to person. People were arrested and beaten for their involvement in that movement, yet it could not be stopped and it changed America ever.

That is the kind of fight that all Americans need to be willing to engage in now. The Civil Rights Movement was an American movement. But without personal interaction and communication, that movement would have fallen apart and caved in to the pressure. If we are going to save the American Dream for this generation, or at least restore the American Dream for the next generation, we must keep the lines between entertainment and news clear

WHEN AMERICANS DON'T PARTICIPATE IN THE GOVERNMENT, THE AMERICAN DREAM IS AT RISK.

and un-blurred. When the minds of learned people become confused, confused people become apathetic, and apathetic people do not participate in government. When Americans don't participate in the government, the American Dream is at risk.

A Higher Standard

We need to hold our journalists to a higher standard. We must reinforce their contribution to protecting and ensuring the liberties that we enjoy. It is only through a responsible press corps that Americans will once again begin to trust the inner workings of our government system. I am not naïve enough to believe that this will happen overnight; its deterioration did not happen overnight. However, there is no time better than now to begin to turn things around.

Further, we must hold our elected officials to a higher standard as well. They must begin to distinguish between entertainment and leadership. When an elected official becomes enamored with the cameras or media attention, they lose credibility as a leader. The lines have become so blurred between entertainers and leaders, that it is very difficult to tell one from the other. We expect that former athletes and retired coaches will become sports commentators and journalists. It actually enhances our experience of the game to be guided by experts. However, when we see former political leaders becoming journalists or commentators, is very difficult for us to trust their voice or opinion as being unbiased.

Mass media and Madison Avenue are not solely responsible for the blurring of the lines. The market has been driven by demand and the fascination we have with sensationalism. In addition to demanding more of our leaders, we must demand more of ourselves as citizens. We must learn the difference between reality and fantasy if we are going to protect the American Dream. Admittedly, there are times when we prefer the fantasy version versus the truth, and will even pay more for the fantasy. But in the end, deceptive fantasies will only rob us of the American Dream. In this age of real-time media and instant messaging we have to know that there are sources who will give us an accurate, up-to-date description of exactly what is taking place. "Then you will know the truth, and the truth will set you free," (John 8:32 NIV).

CHAPTER 12

RESTORING THE DREAM

*"This country will not be a good place for
any of us to live in unless we make it
a good place for all of us to live in."*

—THEODORE ROOSEVELT

In order to restore the American Dream, we must restore
faith and hope in democracy. We must give Americans the
belief that once again our lawmakers can be trusted and our
laws will be equally enforced. Unfortunately this is not a
commonly held belief at this time. We must also see

Americans go back to work. According to recently released nationwide numbers, 9.5% of our citizens are unemployed. That number, in fact, is deceiving. What it really means in lay terms is that, of the 10 people who want to work, one person can't find a job. But, actually, the reality is worse. In New York's 15th Congressional District, it is estimated that as many as 50% of black and Latino men between the ages of 18 and 35 currently are unemployed. There are so many people that have given up trying to find work and are ready to settle for public assistance. Something has to change.

Throughout the Bible, we are reminded of the intrinsic value of work for both the individual and the community. The book of Proverbs tells us, "The laborer's appetite works for him; his hunger drives him on," (Proverbs 16:26 NIV). Americans understand this and have always shared a strong work ethic. That is why our current financial situation is so debilitating and crippling. It has not only robbed us of the right to earn a living, but also of the personal dignity that accompanies our efforts. The promise of work is the foundation of the American Dream. Without this foundation, our economy will not recover no matter how many stimulus dollars are dumped into it. The American economy is driven largely by consumers. If the consumers are unable to purchase goods or services, then our economy will screech to halt.

The Talmud (rabbinical commentary on the Jewish Law) explains that the highest form of charity is to give in such a way as to affirm a person's dignity, worth, and value. This means that it is much more valuable to give a person a job than a check for not working. Most of us would agree that it is equally important to help those in our nation who truly cannot do for themselves. But we are rapidly becoming a nation that is more dependant on entitlement programs from the federal government than on a free-market economy to sustain its citizens.

The American Dream cannot be given to citizens by the government. The role of government is simply to insure that each citizen has equal access to life, liberty, and the pursuit of happiness. The government cannot be the source of life, liberty or happiness. If we are truly going to restore the American Dream then we must begin to refocus the role of government and create meaningful private sector employment.

★ THE
★ GOVERNMENT
★ CANNOT BE
★ THE SOURCE
★ OF LIFE, LIBERTY
★ OR HAPPINESS.

Looking Forward

"For the past 50 years, the United States has been a job creator—or has it? We have created 80 million jobs since 1960. During the sixties, we created almost 20 million jobs. The same thing happened in the seventies, the eighties, and the nineties. But something terrible happened in the last decade. We lost jobs. And in this new decade, we are still losing jobs. We are losing jobs in spite of the massive amounts of money that we are pumping into the public sector to create jobs. We cannot afford to have another decade where jobs are lost," (Chuck Vollmer, *Jobenomics; A Plan for America*).

Jobenomics is a plan to create 20 million private sector jobs by 2020. The money that is generated to pay the people in both the private and public sectors comes from the private sector—from large, medium, and small businesses. Small businesses provide the most growth and the most promise. We need to do all that we can to see to it that our small businesses are not discouraged, but encouraged to thrive.

OUR AIM IS TO CREATE 50,000 NEW PRIVATE-SECTOR JOBS IN HARLEM.

Jobenomics has been designed by private business people to teach individuals to achieve personal freedom and dignity through finding and maintaining meaningful work. This program is being launched in Harlem in September 2010. Our aim is to create 50,000 new private-sector jobs in Harlem. We will provide mentoring from established coaches and successful individuals. We have also secured relationships with various lending institutions to assist qualified businesses to receive the loans that will help them grow. Finally, we plan to create incubators for small businesses where teams of experts can assist in producing quality business plans and even some early sales. These teams will generate ideas for growth and partnerships.

The American Dream needs to be restored through actions aimed at recovering trust and faith in democracy. Americans cannot and must not trust their government to redistribute wealth. We will not trust our government to provide jobs and economic security. The reason we must never trust the government for these things is because our government cannot provide or pay for these things. The Constitution of the United States gives Congress the power to regulate commerce. This regulation clause gives Congress the ability to regulate for fair trade agreements. But when the government ventures beyond fair trade it actually serves to hinder businesses rather than to encourage them.

Restoring the American Dream is going to require action that will bring entrepreneurs to the table. The role of government leaders is to be the catalyst connector for these entrepreneurs and best business practices. Once sound business practices have been established in a market-driven economy, we will ensure that both job creation and the restoration of the American Dream can reach its full potential.

CHAPTER 13

THE IMPORTANCE OF HARLEM

"One belongs to New York instantly, one belongs
to it as much in five minutes as in five years."

—THOMAS WOLFE

I've already mentioned how, following my stint with the New York Jets, I was drawn to New York City as the place to answer my calling to work in inner-city ministries. In retrospect, I realize there was another reason why I was drawn to New York City. It has always been the beacon and launching point of the American Dream for countless immigrants.

The inscription on the Statue of Liberty reads, *"Give me your tired, your poor, your huddled masses yearning to breathe free, the wretched refuse of your teeming shore. Send these, the homeless, tempest-tossed to me. I lift my lamp beside the golden door."* For people worldwide, the Statue of Liberty is one of the most recognizable icons of the United States and all that it stands for—especially the opportunities of the American Dream. For many years, it was one of the first glimpses of the United States for millions of immigrants and visitors after ocean voyages from around the world.

HARLEM IS SIGNIFICANT BOTH BECAUSE IT IS IN NEW YORK AND BECAUSE OF ITS CONTRIBUTIONS AS A COMMUNITY TO THE SOCIAL AND CULTURAL LIFE OF NEW YORK CITY, THE UNITED STATES, AND THE WORLD.

Harlem is significant both because it is in New York and because of its contributions as a community to the social and cultural life of New York City, the United States, and the World—especially to its African-American, Caribbean, and Hispanic populations—for decades. The poetry, art, music, food, and religious communities have continued to give Harlem its rich cultural underpinning. Still, to this day, on Sunday mornings many of the larger churches are packed with busloads of tourists that are coming to get a taste of the Harlem sound and the African-American experience.

THE IMPORTANCE OF HARLEM
★ ★ ★

While Harlem recently has experienced a great Renaissance, and at the same time is now experiencing great gentrification, it also represents the epicenter for what I consider the robbery of the American Dream. While it now has incredible prices on new homes, it also has public housing and pockets of institutional poverty that have existed for decades—and is not likely to go away anytime soon. Harlem has no shortage of rags to riches stories. Both legitimate and illegitimate entrepreneurs have always been able to achieve their piece of the American Dream in Harlem with hard work and ingenuity.

But the political climate in Harlem has been in a steady state of deterioration for the past 40 years. I say this not because its congressional seat has been occupied by one person for that period of time, but rather because of the mindset that has taken hold of the hearts of the residents here. Adam Clayton Powell Jr., the first African-American representative from Harlem, represented this area in the House of Representatives from 1937 to 1970. During that time he was a consummate champion for civil rights in addition to being a pastor and a historical icon.

When Powell reached the pinnacle of his career, his lifestyle choices and swagger began to be an impediment to his leadership and representation. Thus Charles B. Rangel unseated him in 1970. The House of Representatives was designed to give the people a choice every two years. But when one political establishment or machine takes office and begins to immediately eliminate competition in order to sustain its own power base, it becomes a threat to the American Dream. The black community is by no means the first to experience this. Harlem suffers more than most from this phenomenon because of the great visibility and cultural realities of Harlem and the flamboyance of its leaders.

The socioeconomic realities of Harlem do not reflect the passing on of the American Dream. Harlem's citizens have voted less in recent elections than any other community in Manhattan. Harlem still has the lowest family-per-capita income of any other community in Manhattan apart from the lower East side. The majority of the attendees at Harlem's churches do not live in Harlem.

Harlem is experiencing a catastrophic drain of its greatest minds and future leaders. Many of its best and brightest are working elsewhere and eventually moving elsewhere. Many of the workers who do raise their families in Harlem are retiring and relocating to the South for it's lower cost of living and vibrant community life. Even worse, most of the businesses in Harlem are not owned by people who live in Harlem.

In spite of these issues, Harlem politics reflect some of the same "clubhouse politics" that take place in Chicago, Philadelphia, and any other big city or community. We have an elite group of people who have a philosophical bent and private interests and enterprises, all of which dissuades political involvement on the part of new people coming into the mix. Longtime Harlem Congressman Charlie Rangel is still popular in Harlem because he's an icon, not necessarily because he's served the best interests of Harlem.

A Cry for Change

As Americans, we have gotten lazy. We don't hold our elected officials to the same standards that they were elected to uphold. Harlem is a prime example of what happens when "we the people" abrogate our responsibility to hold our leaders accountable to serve the community first and foremost. I walked around Harlem during the last mayoral election asking people if they were going to vote. The overwhelming majority that I encountered said that they were not going to vote. When I asked them why, they replied that their vote didn't matter. They were uninspired.

We have grown too complacent. We believe that there are laws that stop people from being corrupt and that those laws are sufficient to protect us if they become "too corrupt."

But when corrupt politicians and leaders aren't called to the carpet, the rest of us become complacent, disenfranchised, and give up on the American Dream. The truth is that unless we hold elected officials, government employees, and other leaders accountable for their actions, they can and will break the law.

HARLEM AND WASHINGTON HEIGHTS NEEDS A RENAISSANCE— A REBIRTH OF THE INDIVIDUAL PURSUIT OF THE AMERICAN DREAM.

Harlem and Washington Heights needs a renaissance—a rebirth of the individual pursuit of the American Dream. We need to climb out of our Internet chat rooms and join together as a community to actively pursue the American Dream and help our neighbors do the same. When we do not gather as a community, we lose touch with who we are and diminish the very type of human interaction that is required for democracy to function at peak efficiency.

My entire professional life has centered on the development of leaders. I was personally the beneficiary of many gifted and amazing mentors. Each was flawed in a way and yet driven to make a difference by imparting whatever wisdom they had to the younger generation. Attending Virginia Tech, a land grant university, instilled in me the value of education for the sake of collective advance and not just elitism.

That is why I believe that there is no greater time or opportunity for me to enter the public dialogue to fight for the soul of democracy than the present. The urgency of this hour cannot be overstated. I feel called to help raise up a new generation of leaders to fight for democracy in much the same way that each generation has had to fight—whether against external or internal threats to our way of life.

The Problems at Hand . . .

The problems that are facing our nation and the urgency that is needed to resolve them cannot be overstated. We find ourselves living in a period in history in which we have become more individualistic and separated by self-interest than ever before. It is also a time in which we need to be united and rally around the common causes of freedom, liberty, and democracy. Our separation is caused in no small part by technology and the very individual liberties that we have come to appreciate. What we have failed to instill in this generation is an understanding that these liberties that we so readily enjoy have been bought with a price. And that price must be paid forward by each generation.

New York's 15th congressional district faces double-digit unemployment, while at the same time this district has been the supposed recipient of mass amounts of federal spending toward the "empowerment zone." We need jobs now, through small business stimulus and tax relief. We also need a renewed commitment to strengthening small businesses and entrepreneurs in this community.

We need education for the masses. We need education that uses the existing public infrastructure as well as attracting private resources directed toward educating the most disadvantaged of this community. Recent statistics have told us that there are approximately 200,000 young people between the ages of 18 and 25 living in this community who do not have a high school diploma. This, by the way, is the same group of people who are most likely to enter the criminal justice system.

We have a president in office and an administration that believes that the Federal Government is the panacea for all the problems facing America. I believe that this conviction and the practices associated with it are leading us into an era of unprecedented dependence on a bloated federal government. The real problem with over-dependence on the Federal Government is that their involvement has reached far beyond the scope of what we as Americans have elected them to do. As a result our government is rapidly encroaching on the liberties that we enjoy.

Our government has chosen to encumber us and countless future generations with a mammoth piece of healthcare legislation, despite the vast majority of Americans' disapproval. In my opinion, the intent was never about improving our nation's health, but about money. The conversation never ventured into how to make Americans healthier, but rather who was responsible and who was going to pay for it. Never, during the entire course of the health care debate, did the facts emerge that as a nation we spend more on health coverage than any of the 17 industrialized nations of the world. At the same time we are the sickest of all of said nations. Certainly, we do need to address healthcare issues, but we need to find ways to stimulate healthier living rather than merely shifting the blame and allowing the federal government to take over healthcare. I have said numerous times that the federal government cannot run government, much less a business, especially one that is as complicated as healthcare.

What Am I Going to Do?

This brings me to the critical question: What am I going to do about it? My plan for resolving these issues or at least addressing them in a comprehensive manner is to run for the Congress of the United States of America. I believe that through the consistent engagement of the electorate that we will find a shift in opinion and give a voice to the voiceless. I believe that when those who have not been heard are able to rise and speak and be empowered to regain control of their government, things will change. It is imperative that we have common citizens run for elected office. It is important that common citizens gain these offices and restore power to the people.

My purpose for running is to engage in a public dialogue and debate and bring common sense values back to the discussion. We want to see the role of citizen legislature restored to the people of New York's 15th congressional district. As Abraham Lincoln once said, "The probability that we may fall in the struggle ought not to deter us from the support of a cause we believe to be just; it shall not deter me."

When elected, my work begins in earnest and it will be an uphill battle. People will need to be healed of their distress and distrust of government. I do not expect this to occur immediately, but I am confident that over a period of time the confidence and faith of our American people can be restored.

ALTHOUGH THE COST IS GREAT AND THE REWARD NOT CERTAIN, THE CAUSE IS WORTHY.

I can honestly say that I have never entered into any endeavor that has been as costly as the one that I have engaged in. And quite honestly I feel equally that, although the cost is great and the reward not certain, the cause is worthy.

What we will need to accomplish this task is nothing short of our lives and liberty—no less than our forebears have laid on the line to bring us this far. We need to be willing to give our time, talent, and treasure toward this purpose. Without it we will continue to suffer through generation after generation of lethargic voters and greedy representatives. But *you* are part of the solution for this problem. Together we can make a change. Together we can make a difference. To do nothing is not an option because our failure to act is tantamount to stealing the American Dream.

Make your voice heard and do your part to protect the future of the American Dream.

To contact your U.S. Senator, visit:
http://www.senate.gov/general/contact_information/senators_cfm.cfm

To contact your U.S. Representative, visit:
http://www.house.gov/house/MemberWWW_by_State.shtml

To contact your state legislators, visit:
http://www.ncsl.org/?tabid=17173

ENDNOTES

1 Adams, J.T. (1933). *The Epic of America*. Little Brown & Company.

2 Official home of the American tea party movement. (2010). Retrieved from http://teapartypatriots.ning.com/.

3 About SBA. Retrieved from http://www.sba.gov/aboutsba/index.html.

4 *The Forum* at The Online Library of Liberty. http://oll.liberty-fund.org/.

5 Hymowitz, K.S. (2005, Summer). *The Black Family: 40 Years of Lies*. Retrieved from http://www.freerepublic.com/focus/f-news/1450339/posts.

6 *Thomas Jefferson Encyclopedia*. Retrieved from http://wiki.monti-cello.org/.